N i n t h   E d i t i o n

THE
WASHINGTON
NOTARY LAW
PRIMER

*All the hard-to-find information
every Washington Notary Public
needs to know!*

National Notary Association

Published by:

National Notary Association Press
9350 De Soto Ave., P.O. Box 2402
Chatsworth, CA 91313-2402
Telephone: (818) 739-4000
FAX: (818) 700-0920
E-mail: nna@nationalnotary.org
www.NationalNotary.org

The information in this *Primer* is correct and current at the time
of its publication, although new laws, regulations and rulings may
subsequently affect the validity of certain sections. This information
is provided to aid comprehension of state Notary Public requirements
and should not be construed as legal advice. Please consult an
attorney for inquiries relating to legal matters.

Ninth Edition
First Edition © 1986

ISBN Number: 1-59767-046-4
L.C. Control Number: 2005928993

Table of Contents

Introduction 1

How to Become a Washington Notary Public 3

Tools of the Trade 6

10 Most-Asked Questions 8

Steps to Proper Notarization 13

Notary Laws Explained 18
   The Notary Commission 18
   Official Notarial Acts 22
   Practices and Procedures 38
   Misconduct, Fines and Penalties 63

Digital Signatures 69

Test Your Knowledge 71

Washington Laws Pertaining to Notaries Public 77

Office of the Washington Department of Licensing. 108

Bureaus of Vital Statistics 109

Hague Convention Nations 113

About the NNA 116

Index 118

Introduction

You are to be commended on your interest in Washington Notary law! Purchasing *The Washington Notary Law Primer* identifies you as a conscientious professional who takes his or her official duties seriously.

In few fields is the expression "more to it than meets the eye" truer than in Notary law. What often appears on the surface to be a simple procedure may have important legal considerations.

The purpose of *The Washington Notary Law Primer* is to provide you with a resource to help you understand the many complex laws that affect notarization. In so doing, the *Primer* will acquaint you with all of the important aspects of Washington Notary law and with prudent notarial practices in general.

This edition of *The Washington Notary Law Primer* contains recent law changes taking effect in 2008, including the enactment of the Uniform Real Property Electronic Recording Act, which enables a recording officer to accept electronic real property documents for recording in conformance with technical standards set by the Washington Secretary of State.

While *The Washington Notary Law Primer* begins with informative chapters on how to obtain your appointment, what tools the Notary needs, often-asked questions and critical steps in notarization, the heart of this book is the chapter entitled "Notary Laws Explained." Here, we take you through the myriad of Notary laws and put them in easy-to-understand terms. Every pertinent section of the law is explained, as are topics not covered by Washington law but nonetheless of vital concern to you as a Notary.

For handy reference, we have reprinted the complete text of the Washington statutes that relate to the Notary Public's duties. In addition, we have included the addresses and telephone numbers of the Washington Department of Licensing office and Bureaus of Vital Statistics, plus a list of nations that are parties to the Hague Convention, a treaty that simplifies the process of authentication.

Whether you are about to be appointed for the first time or are a longtime Notary, we are sure that *The Washington Notary Law Primer* will provide you with new insight and understanding.

Milton G. Valera
President
National Notary Association

How to Become a Washington Notary Public

1. Ensure that you comply with the basic qualifications for a Washington Notary appointment.

First, you must be a legal resident of the state or a resident of an adjoining state and work or conduct business in Washington. Second, you must be 18 years of age or older. Third, you must not have been convicted of a serious crime. Fourth, you must not have had any previous Notary appointment or professional license revoked in Washington or any other state. And fifth, you must be able to read and write the English language.

U.S. citizenship is not required as long as you legally reside in this country under federal law. There is also no minimum time of state residency — you can apply for an appointment on the same day that you enter Washington.

2. Obtain an appointment application form.

You can obtain the official application and information packet for a Washington Notary appointment from the Department of Licensing by calling (360) 664-1550. You may also obtain an application in person or through the mail from:

>Department of Licensing
>Notary Public Licensing Program
>P.O. Box 9048
>Olympia, WA 98507-9048

The application and other information are also available via the Internet at www.dol.wa.gov/unfc/notfront.htm. From this site, you can request an application via e-mail or download the form directly to your computer.

3. Complete the application form.

Read the entire application packet, and complete all of the questions, typing or printing neatly in ink. Be aware that any misstatement or omission of information may be cause for denial or later revocation of your Notary appointment.

Your application must be endorsed by three people who are at least 18 years old, unrelated to you and eligible to vote in Washington.

If you are seeking reappointment as a Notary before your current appointment expires, send the Department a letter of request with your name, address and date of birth, accompanied by a new $10,000 surety bond and a renewal fee of $30. You do not need to obtain the endorsers' signatures again.

However, if you are seeking reappointment as a Notary after your appointment has expired, you must follow the same procedures as if applying for the first time.

4. Take your oath.

The Notary application will feature a personal declaration containing an oath of office. Go to a Notary Public, sign your appointment application in his or her presence and take your oath. Be sure to sign your name exactly as it is to appear on your Certificate of Appointment.

5. Obtain your bond.

A $10,000 bond is required for Washington Notaries. Contact an insurance company authorized to issue surety bonds in Washington. The bond must cover your entire four-year Notary term. All spaces on the bond must be completed, and the name and signature on the bond must be identical to the name and signature on the application.

6. Submit the application with the appropriate fee and your Notary bond.

The completed and signed application, bond and $30 fee payable to "Washington State Treasurer" must be mailed or delivered to the Department of Licensing, Notary Public Section, at the address on page 3.

Renewing Notaries will receive a new appointment number and expiration date, and will be required to obtain a new seal or stamp. The new seal or stamp may not be used until the effective date on the new Certificate of Appointment.

7. Obtain an official Notary seal or stamp.

Once your application has been approved, the Division of Licensing will send you your official Notary Certificate of Appointment. Submit a copy of the Certificate to a company of your choice in order to purchase a Notary seal or stamp. See "Notary Seal or Stamp" on pages 49-51 for the specific requirements of Washington law regarding a Notary seal or stamp.

Once you have purchased your seal or stamp and journal, and once you have reached the effective date specified on your Certificate of Appointment, you are ready to notarize. ■

Tools
of the Trade

Notaries need several tools in order to carry out their duties lawfully and efficiently. These tools are as important to the Notary as a hammer and saw are to the carpenter.

Inking Stamp

The inked rubber stamp affixes a photographically reproducible impression in indelible ink. It is a convenient, official seal for notarizing documents that will be submitted to a public recorder for microfilming. The Washington Notary's stamp must meet numerous specific standards. (See "Notary Seal or Stamp," pages 49-51.)

Seal Embosser

The embosser may be used by itself as an official Washington Notary seal. However, when an embosser is affixed on documents that will be publicly recorded and microfilmed (deeds, etc.), the resulting impression must be smudged with ink, graphite or carbon to become photographically reproducible. When used in conjunction with an inking stamp, the embossment need not be smudged. Many Notaries also emboss pages and certificates together as a fraud deterrent. Because photocopies of documents can easily pass as originals, the embossment can be used to distinguish an original from a photocopy.

Journal of Notarial Acts

Though Washington law does not require Notaries to keep a record of their official acts, the National Notary Association encourages such recordkeeping by every Notary.

The Notary's journal provides a record of notarial transactions that may be used as evidence in court proceedings. It is the best protection for a Notary accused of misconduct.

Bound Notary journals with numbered pages have proven to be the safest and most fraud-resistant type of record book. Loose-leaf books are the least secure.

Jurat Stamp

The jurat stamp impresses on an affidavit the jurat wording, "Subscribed and sworn to before me this _____ day of _____ (month), _____ (year) by _____." The jurat stamp is more convenient (and safer, since critical wording will not be omitted) than typing the wording on each affidavit.

Venue Stamp

The venue stamp is used in conjunction with the jurat stamp in a jurat. The phrase "State of _____, County of _____" indicates where the jurat was executed. The stamp may also be used for acknowledgments.

Fingerprinting Device

Though not required by law, asking a signer to leave a thumbprint in the Notary's journal is a strong deterrent to forgery. Small, inexpensive devices make taking a print easy.

Notarial Certificates

Preprinted notarial certificates for acknowledgments, jurats and copy certification are available.

Errors and Omissions Insurance

Notary errors and omissions insurance (E&O) provides protection for Notaries who are sued for damages resulting from unintentional notarial mistakes. In the event of a lawsuit, the E&O insurance company will provide and pay for the Notary's legal counsel and absorb any damages levied by a court or agreed to in a settlement, up to the policy coverage limit. Errors and omissions insurance does not cover the Notary for intentional misconduct. ■

As a full-service organization, the National Notary Association makes available to Washington Notaries all notarial items required by law, custom and convenience.

10 Most-Asked Questions

Every Notary has at least a question or two about whether and how to notarize. But certain questions pop up again and again. These top 10 questions are asked repeatedly at the National Notary Association's seminars, its annual National Conference of Notaries Public and through its *Notary Information Service*.

As with most questions about notarization, the answers are not always a simple "yes" or "no" but rather, "it depends ..."

Here is what every Notary wants to know:

1. Can I notarize a will?

It depends. A Notary should only notarize a will if clear instructions and a notarial certificate are provided. If the signer of the will is relying upon the Notary for advice on how to proceed, the Notary should tell the individual to see an attorney.

Laws regarding wills differ from state to state. Some states do not require the notarization of wills, while others allow it as one of several witnessing options. Often, it is not the will itself that is notarized, but accompanying affidavits signed by witnesses.

The danger in notarizing wills is that would-be testators who have drafted their own wills without legal advice may believe that notarization will make their wills legal and valid. However, even when notarized, such homemade wills may be worthless because the testators failed to obtain the proper number of witnesses or omitted important information.

In fact, notarization itself may actually void an otherwise properly executed handwritten (holographic) will, because courts have occasionally held that any writing on the document (other than the testator's) invalidates the will.

2. Can I notarize for a stranger with no identification?

Yes. If identification of a signer cannot be based on personal knowledge or identification documents (ID cards), a Notary may rely on the oath or affirmation of a personally known credible identifying witness to identify an unknown signer.

The Notary must personally know the credible identifying witness, who must personally know the document signer. This establishes a chain of personal knowledge from the Notary to the credible identifying witness to the signer.

A credible identifying witness should be someone the Notary believes to be trustworthy and impartial. A person with a financial or other beneficial interest in a document could not be a reliable witness.

When no credible identifying witness is available to identify a stranger without IDs, and the signer is unable to obtain an adequate identification document, the Notary may have no choice but to tell the signer to find a personally known Notary or a friend who personally knows a Notary.

3. Can I notarize a photograph?

No. To simply stamp and sign a photograph is improper. A Notary's signature and seal must appear only on a notarial certificate (such as an acknowledgment or jurat) accompanying a written statement signed by another person.

However, a signature on a written statement referring to an accompanying or attached photograph may be notarized. If the photograph is large enough, the statement and notarial certificate might even appear on its reverse side. Such a format may be acceptable when notarized photos are requested by persons seeking medical or health licenses, or by permanent legal residents renewing foreign passports.

A word of caution here: A Notary should always be suspicious about notarizing a photo-bearing card or document that could be fraudulently used as a bogus "official" ID.

4. What if there is no room for my seal, or what if it smears?

Usually, if notarial wording printed on a document leaves no room for a seal or stamp, a loose certificate can be attached and filled out instead, as long as the certificate wording is substantially the same as that on the document.

If an initial seal or stamp impression is unreadable and there is ample room on the document, another impression can be affixed nearby. The illegibility of the first impression will indicate why a second seal impression was necessary. The Notary should then record in the journal that a second seal was applied.

A Notary should never attempt to fix an imperfect seal impression with pen, ink or correction fluid. This may be viewed as evidence of tampering and cause the document's rejection by a receiving agency.

5. Can I notarize signatures on photocopies of documents?

Yes. A photocopy may be notarized as long as it bears an original signature, meaning that the photocopy must have been signed with pen and ink. A photocopied signature may never be notarized.

Similarly, a faxed document must be signed in ink. In addition, if a faxed document is on thermal paper (the slick paper used in older fax machines), the document should be photocopied onto regular copy paper in order to avoid both the fading of any printed matter and allow the affixation of signatures and the Notary's seal.

Note that some public recorders will not accept notarized signatures on photocopied documents because they will not adequately reproduce in microfilming.

When carbon copies are made, the Notary will sometimes be asked to conform rather than to notarize the copies. To conform a copy, the Notary reaffixes the official seal or stamp on the copy (carbon will not readily transfer a seal or stamp impression) and writes "Conformed Copy" prominently across the copy.

6. May I notarize for customers only?

No. As a public official, a Notary is not appointed to serve just the customers or clients of any one business, even when the Notary's employer has paid for the bond, appointment fees and notarial supplies. There is no such officer as a "Notary Private."

It is ethically improper — although hardly ever explicitly prohibited by statute — to discriminate between customers and noncustomers in offering or refusing to offer notarial services and in charging or not charging fees.

Discrimination against anyone who presents a lawful request for notarization is not a suitable policy for a public official commissioned to serve all of the public equally. Also, such discrimination can provide the basis for lawsuits.

7. Can I notarize a document in a language I cannot read?

Perhaps. As long as the notarial certificate and document signature are in a language the Notary can read, Washington Notaries are not expressly prohibited from notarizing a document written in a language they cannot read.

However, there are certain difficulties and dangers in doing so. The main difficulty for the Notary is making an accurate journal description of an unreadable document. The main danger is that the document may be blatantly fraudulent. It is always better to refer the signer to a bilingual Notary who can read the language.

Under no circumstances should a notarization be performed if the Notary and the principal signer cannot communicate in the same language.

8. Can I certify a copy of a birth certificate?

No. While Washington Notaries are authorized to certify copies, they should never certify copies of documents that are either public records or publicly recordable.

Only an officer in a bureau of vital statistics should certify a copy of a birth certificate or other vital public record. A Notary's "certification" of a birth or death record may actually lend credibility to a counterfeit or tampered document. Only a county recording official should certify a copy of a deed or other recordable instrument.

Washington Notaries may properly certify copies of original personal papers such as college diplomas, letters and in-house business documents.

9. Does a document have to be signed in my presence?

No and yes. Documents requiring acknowledgments normally do not need to be signed in the Notary's presence. However, the signer must appear before the Notary at the time of notarization to acknowledge that he or she freely signed for the purposes stated in the document.

An acknowledgment certificate indicates that the signer

personally appeared before the Notary, was identified by the Notary, and acknowledged to the Notary that the document was freely signed.

On the other hand, documents requiring a jurat must be signed in the Notary's presence, as dictated by the typical jurat wording, "Subscribed (signed) and sworn to before me ..."

A jurat certificate indicates that the signer personally appeared before the Notary, was positively identified by the Notary, was given an oath or affirmation by the Notary and signed the document in the Notary's presence.

10. Can I notarize for a family member?

Yes and no. Although Washington law does not directly prohibit notarizing for family members, the National Notary Association recommends that a Notary not notarize in these cases. Notaries who do so may violate guidelines prohibiting a direct beneficial interest — especially in notarizing for spouses.

Besides the possibility of a financial interest in notarizing for a relative, there may be an emotional interest that can prevent the Notary from acting impartially. For example, a Notary who is asked to notarize a contract signed by his brother might attempt to persuade the sibling to sign or not sign. As a brother, the individual is entitled to exert influence — but this is entirely improper for a Notary.

Even if a Notary has no direct beneficial interest in the document and does not attempt to influence the signer, notarizing for a relative could subject the document to a legal challenge if other parties to the transaction allege that the Notary could not have acted impartially. ■

Steps to Proper Notarization

If a Notary can convincingly show that he or she used every reasonable precaution expected of a person of ordinary prudence and intelligence, then the Notary has exercised reasonable care — a shield against liability.

What constitutes reasonable care?

The following 14-step checklist will help Notaries apply reasonable care and avoid the most common pitfalls.

1. Require every signer to personally appear.

The signer must appear in person before the Notary on the date and in the county stated in the notarial certificate. Personal appearance means that the signer is in the Notary's physical presence — face to face in the same room. A telephone call does not constitute personal appearance.

2. Make a careful identification.

The Notary should identify every document signer through personal knowledge, the oath or affirmation of a credible identifying witness or reliable identification documents (ID cards).

When using ID cards, the Notary must examine them closely to detect alteration, counterfeiting or evidence that they are issued to an impostor. Do not rely on a type of card with which you are unfamiliar unless you check it against a reference such as the *U.S. Identification Manual* or the *I.D. Checking Guide*.

3. Feel certain the signer understands the transaction.

A conscientious and careful Notary will be certain not only

of the signer's identity and willingness to sign, but also will make a layperson's commonsense judgment about the signer's ability to understand the document.

Screening for willingness — that is, making sure the signer signs the document of his or her own free will — is required if the notarial certificate states that the signer's acknowledgment is "the free act and deed of the signer," or words to that effect.

The Revised Code of Washington specifies that a Notary taking the acknowledgment of a physically challenged signer who cannot sign or make a mark and who directs the Notary to sign on his or her behalf must determine that the signer is otherwise capable of entering into the transaction.

While Washington law does not expressly require the Notary to make a judgment about the signer's ability to understand the transaction in all other cases, it is in the Notary's best interest to do so. A document signer who is not able to respond intelligibly in a simple conversation with the Notary should not be considered able to sign at that moment.

If in doubt, the Notary can ask the signer if he or she understands the document and can explain its purpose. Or, if in a medical environment, the signer's doctor can be consulted.

4. Check the signature.

The Notary must make sure that the document signer signs the same name appearing on the identification presented.

To check for possible forgery, the Notary should compare the signature that the person leaves in the journal of notarial acts against the signatures on the document and on the IDs. Also, it should be noted whether the signer appears to be laboring to make the journal signature, a possible indication of forgery in progress.

Generally, an abbreviated form of a name (John D. Smith instead of John David Smith, for example) is acceptable. However, deviation is only allowed if the individual is signing with less than and not more than what is on the identification document.

5. Look for blank spaces.

Although not expressly prohibited by Washington law, notarization of incomplete documents is unwise.

Documents with blank spaces have a great potential for fraudulent misuse. A borrower, for example, might sign an incomplete promissory note, trusting the lender to fill it out, only to discover later that the lender has written in an amount in excess of what was actually borrowed.

If the blanks are inapplicable and intended to be left unfilled, the signer may be asked to line through each space (using ink), or to write in "Not Applicable" or "N/A."

6. Scan the document.

Notaries are not required to read the documents they notarize. However, they should note certain important particulars about a document, such as its title, for recording in the journal of notarial acts. Notaries may also count and record the number of pages; this can show whether pages are later fraudulently added or removed.

7. Check the document's date.

For acknowledgments, the date of signing on the document must either precede or be the same as the date of the notarization, but not follow it. For a jurat or signature witnessing, the document signing date and the notarization date must be the same.

A document dated to follow the date on its notarial certificate risks rejection by a recorder, who may question how the document could have been notarized before it was signed.

8. Keep a journal of notarial acts.

While not required by Washington law, a journal record is a vital part of any notarial act. If a notarized document is lost or altered, or if certain facts about the transaction are later challenged, the Notary's journal becomes valuable evidence. It can protect the rights of all parties to a transaction and help Notaries defend themselves against false accusations.

The Notary should include all of the pertinent details of the notarization in the journal: The date, time and type of notarization; the date and type of document; the printed name and address of the signer (and any witnesses); the way in which this person was identified and the notarial fees charged, if any. In addition, any other pertinent data, such as the representative capacity the signer is claiming, may be entered. Signers may also be asked to leave a signature and/or a thumbprint in the Notary's journal as a deterrent to fraud, though this is not required by law in Washington.

9. Complete the journal entry first.

The Notary should complete the journal entry before filling out the notarial certificate. This prevents a signer from leaving before the important public record of the notarization is made in the journal.

10. Make sure the document has notarial wording.

If a notarial certificate does not come with the document, the Notary must ask the document signer what type of notarization — acknowledgment, jurat or other — is required. The Notary may then type the appropriate notarial wording on the document or attach a preprinted, loose certificate.

If the signer does not know what type of notarization is required, he or she should contact the document's issuing or receiving agency to determine this. This decision is never the Notary's to make unless the Notary is also an attorney or an appropriately trained expert. (See "Selecting Certificates," page 46.)

11. Be attentive to details.

When filling out the certificate, the Notary must make sure the venue correctly identifies the place of notarization. If the venue is preprinted and incorrect, the Notary must line through the incorrect state and/or county, write in the proper site of the notarization and initial and date the change.

Also, the Notary must pay attention to spaces on the notarial certificate that indicate the number and gender of the document signers, as well as how they were identified — for example, leave the plural "(s)" untouched or cross it out, as appropriate.

12. Affix your signature and seal or stamp properly.

Notaries should sign exactly the same name appearing on their commissioning papers. And they must never forget to affix their official seals or stamps — a common reason for rejection of a document by a recorder.

The seal or stamp should be placed as close to the Notary's signature as possible without overlapping it. To prevent illegibility, a notarial seal should not be affixed over wording, particularly over a signature.

13. Attach loose certificates correctly.

Recording laws in Washington require that loose Notary certificates be treated and attached like other document pages. Attached certificates should be the same size as the other pages in the document and provide a margin of at least one inch on all sides. A loose certificate page should immediately follow a document's signature page.

Notaries can protect against the removal of loose certificates by embossing them together with the documents and writing the particulars of the document to which the certificate is attached. For example, the notation "Certificate attached to a 15-page partnership agreement between John Smith and Mary Doe, signed December 15, 2007" would deter fraudulent removal and reattachment of a loose certificate.

14. Do not give advice.

Every state prohibits nonattorneys from practicing law. Notaries should never prepare or complete documents for others, or give advice on any matter relating to a document unless they are attorneys or professionals certified or licensed in a relevant area of expertise. The nonattorney Notary never chooses the type of certificate or notarization a document needs, since this decision can have important legal ramifications. The Notary could be held liable for any damages resulting from an incorrectly chosen certificate or notarization. ■

Notary Laws Explained

In layperson's language, this chapter discusses and clarifies key parts of the laws of Washington that regulate Notaries Public. Most of these laws are reprinted in full in "Washington Laws Pertaining to Notaries Public," beginning on page 77.

Most provisions cited are from Chapter 42.44, "Notaries Public," of the Revised Code of Washington (RCW). Other notarial rules are cited from Chapter 308-30, "Notaries Public," of the Washington Administrative Code (WAC).

THE NOTARY COMMISSION

Application for Commission

Qualifications. To become a Notary in Washington, the applicant must (RCW 42.44.020 and 42.44.030):

- Be at least 18 years old.

- Be a legal resident of Washington, or a resident of an adjoining state and regularly working or conducting business in Washington.

- Be able to read and write the English language.

- Not have had a Notary appointment or other professional license revoked in Washington or any other state.

- Not have been convicted of a felony or serious crime involving moral turpitude, misrepresentation, fraud or similar offense.

In addition, the applicant must properly complete and submit the Notary application, including the endorsements and personal declaration, and pay the required fees. (See "Personal Declaration," page 20.)

Endorsements Required. Each application must be endorsed by three state residents who are unrelated to the applicant, are 18 years of age or older and are eligible to vote in Washington. The endorsements must be supplied on the application form.

Endorsements are not required for a person applying for reappointment as long as the person submits the application for reappointment before the current appointment expires (RCW 42.44.070).

Application Fee. The total fee for a Notary appointment applicant is $30, payable to the "Washington State Treasurer" (WAC 308-30-100).

Rejection of Application. The Department of Licensing may deny a Notary application for reasons that include (RCW 42.44.030):

- Failure to meet commission qualifications.

- A false statement knowingly made in the application.

- A conviction for a felony or a crime involving moral turpitude, misrepresentation, fraud or similar offense.

- Revocation, suspension or restriction of another professional license in Washington or any other state.

- Engaging in official misconduct, whether or not criminal penalties resulted.

- Performing a notarial act with gross negligence.

Notary Bond

Required. Washington Notaries are required to obtain a $10,000 surety bond (RCW 42.44.020).

Filing the Bond. The bond must be submitted with the Notary Public application (RCW 42.44.020).

Surety. The required Notary bond must be issued by a licensed bonding or insurance company. The dates on the bond must coincide exactly with the dates of the Notary's four-year term (RCW 42.44.020).

Purpose. The Notary bond protects the public from a Notary's misconduct or negligence. The bond does not protect the Notary, who is liable for all damages resulting from illegal or improper performance of notarial duties.

The bond's surety company agrees to pay damages totalling up to the bond amount to persons who suffer financially because of the Notary's improper acts — intentional or not — in the event that the Notary does not have the money to pay these damages. The surety will seek compensation from the Notary for any damages it has to pay out on the Notary's behalf.

Liable for All Damages. A Notary and the surety company bonding the Notary may be sued by any person who has been damaged by the Notary's official acts. The surety is liable only up to the amount of the bond, but a Notary may be found liable for any amount of money.

Personal Declaration

Requirement. Each prospective Notary must take and sign the personal declaration on the application in the presence of a Notary Public or other person authorized to administer oaths in Washington. A Notary applicant cannot notarize his or her own personal declaration (RCW 42.44.020).

Jurisdiction

Statewide. Notaries may perform official acts throughout the state of Washington but not beyond state borders. Notaries may not witness a signing outside Washington and then return to the state to notarize. All parts of a notarial act must be performed at the same time and place within the state (RCW 42.44.060).

Term of Office

Four-Year Term. A Washington Notary Public's term of office is four years, beginning on the effective date specified on the Certificate of Appointment and ending at midnight on the appointment expiration date (RCW 42.44.060).

Resignation

Purpose. A person must officially resign the notarial appointment if (RCW 42.44.020, 42.44.170 and WAC 308-30-150):

- The person no longer wants to serve out the remainder of the appointment.

- The person no longer lives in or maintains a business or place of employment in Washington.

- The person can no longer read or write English.

- The person is found legally incompetent by judicial ruling.

Procedure. To resign, a Notary must submit written notice and the stamp or seal to the Department of Licensing (RCW 42.44.170 and WAC 308-30-040).

If a notarial journal is maintained by the Notary, state officials direct the Notary to retain the journal for as long as the Notary is subject to potential legal action under the statute of limitations.

Change of Address

Notify Department of Licensing. Whenever a Notary changes his or her address, the Notary must inform the Department of Licensing of the address change. The notice should include the Notary's name, appointment number and the old and new addresses. There is no fee to file a change of address (WAC 308-30-060).

Moving Out of State. If a Notary moves his or her residence — or, if a commuting nonresident, his or her place of employment — out of Washington, he or she vacates the office of Notary. Such a move requires the Notary to resign the appointment (RCW 42.44.020 and WAC 308-30-150). (See "Resignation," above.)

Change of Name

Procedure. When a Notary changes his or her name, the Notary must notify the Department of Licensing in writing. The notification must be accompanied by a bond rider from the Notary's bonding company and a $15 fee for a duplicate Notary

Certificate of Appointment showing the new name
(WAC 308-30-060 and 308-30-100).

New Seal Required. When a Notary files a name change with
the Department of Licensing, he or she will receive a duplicate
Notary Certificate showing the new name. The Notary must
present a copy of the certificate to a qualified seal manufacturer
in order to purchase a new seal or stamp (WAC 308-30-010).

Exception. State officials allow Notaries who are within a few
months of renewal to wait until they renew their commission to
change their name on the application.

OFFICIAL NOTARIAL ACTS

Authorized Acts
Notaries may perform the following official acts
(RCW 42.44.010 and 42.44.080):

- Acknowledgments, certifying that a signer personally
  appeared before the Notary, was identified by the Notary and
  acknowledged freely signing the document. (See pages 23-28.)

- Certified Copies, certifying that a photocopy of an original
  document is true and complete. (See pages 28-29.)

- Depositions, certifying that the spoken words of a witness
  were accurately taken down in writing. Although Notaries
  are authorized to take them, depositions are typically
  performed by skilled court reporters. (See page 30.)

- Oaths and Affirmations, which are solemn promises to a
  Supreme Being (oaths) or solemn promises on one's own
  personal honor (affirmations). (See pages 30-32.)

- Verifications Upon Oath or Affirmation, as found in
  depositions and affidavits, certifying that the signer
  personally appeared before the Notary, was positively
  identified, took an oath or affirmation and signed a written
  statement in the Notary's presence. (See pages 32-33.)

- Witnessing Signatures, certifying that a signer personally appeared before the Notary, was positively identified and signed the document in the Notary's presence. (See pages 33-34.)

- Proofs of Acknowledgment by Subscribing Witness. Although Washington notarial law does not address the use of proofs of execution, state officials say that Notaries may perform this type of act but should proceed with caution. (See pages 34-35.)

- Certifying an Event or Act, certifying that an event or act has occurred or has been performed. (See pages 35-36.)

- Protests, certifying that a negotiable instrument or other written promise to pay was not honored. (See pages 36-38.)

Unauthorized Acts

Notarizing Own Signature. Notaries are not permitted to notarize their own signatures (RCW 42.44.080).

Marriages. Washington Notaries are not authorized to perform marriages unless they are also members of the clergy or officials authorized to solemnize marriages.

Testimonials or Endorsements. A Notary may not use the official Notary seal or the title "Notary Public" to endorse or promote any product or service (WAC 308-30-160).

Telephone Notarizations. Notarizations over the telephone are forbidden. Washington law stipulates that a document signer must personally appear before the Notary at the time of notarization. Notarization based upon a Notary's recognition of a signature without the signer's appearance is not permitted (RCW 42.44.080).

Acknowledgments

A Common Notarial Act. Acknowledgments are one of the most common forms of notarization. Typically, they are executed on deeds and other documents affecting real property that will be publicly recorded by a county auditor.

Purpose. In executing an acknowledgment, the Notary certifies three things (RCW 42.44.080):

1) The signer personally appeared before the Notary on the date and in the county indicated on the notarial certificate. (Notarization cannot be based upon a telephone call or a Notary's familiarity with a signature.)

2) The signer was positively identified by the Notary through personal knowledge or other satisfactory evidence. (See "Identifying Document Signers," pages 38-39.)

3) The signer acknowledged to the Notary that the signature was freely made for the purposes stated in the document. (If a document is willingly signed in the Notary's presence, this act serves as the acknowledgment.)

Signing in Representative Capacity. An individual may acknowledge the signature on a document as a representative of another person (e.g., as an attorney in fact) or of an impersonal legal entity (e.g., as a corporate officer).

The following representative capacities are recognized by Washington law (RCW 42.44.010):

- An authorized officer, agent, partner, trustee or other representative on behalf of a corporation, partnership, trust or other entity

- A public officer, personal representative, guardian or other representative in a capacity specified in the document

- An attorney in fact for a principal signer

- An authorized representative of another person in any other capacity

Proof of Representative Capacity. The Notary is encouraged to ask for proof of a person's authority to sign in a representative capacity. However, an acknowledgment certificate that indicates that the signer took an oath or affirmation declaring that he or she had authority to sign is generally recognized as significant proof of the person's authority to sign as a representative (RCW 42.44.010, 42.44.100 and 64.08.070).

Identifying the Representative Signer. Notaries should identify representative signers as they would any other signer: through personal knowledge, an ID card or the oath of a credible witness. Ideally, the person should also present some type of documentary evidence that shows the person has the authority to sign as a representative.

Certificates for Acknowledgments. Washington law provides wording for acknowledgment certificates that accommodate signers in individual and corporate capacities (RCW 64.08.060 and 64.08.070):

- Certificate of acknowledgment for a person signing as an individual — wording must be substantially as follows:

State of Washington   )
County of _____)

On this day personally appeared before me _____ (name of person appearing), to me known to be the individual, or individuals, described in and who executed the within and foregoing instrument, and acknowledged that he/she/they signed the same as his/her/their free and voluntary act and deed, for the uses and purposes therein mentioned.
Given under my hand and official seal this _____ day of _____ (month), _____ (year).

_____ (Signature of Notary)   (Seal/Stamp of Notary)
Notary Public — State of Washington
My Appointment Expires: _____

- Certificate of acknowledgment for a person signing as a representative of a corporation — wording must be substantially as follows:

State of Washington   )
County of _____)

On this _____ day of _____ (month), _____ (year), before me personally appeared _____ (name of person appearing), to me known to be the _____ (title of corporate officer) of the corporation that executed the within and foregoing instrument, and

acknowledged said instrument to be the free and voluntary act and deed
of said corporation, for the uses and purposes therein mentioned, and
on oath stated that he/she was authorized to execute said instrument
and that the seal affixed is the corporate seal of said corporation.
In Witness Whereof I have hereunto set my hand and affixed my
official seal the day and year first above written.

_____ (Signature of Notary)   (Seal/Stamp of Notary)
Notary Public — State of Washington
My Appointment Expires: _____

Short-Form Certificates. The following short-form
acknowledgment wording may be used in lieu of the lengthier
versions set out on pages 25-26. A Notary may use either the
short-form or long-form versions, depending upon the
circumstances (RCW 42.44.100):

- Certificate of acknowledgment for a person signing as an
  individual — wording must be substantially as follows:

State of Washington   )
County of _____)

I certify that I know or have satisfactory evidence that _____
(name of person) is the person who appeared before me, and said
person acknowledged that he/she signed this instrument and
acknowledged it to be his/her free and voluntary act for the uses and
purposes mentioned in the instrument.
Dated: _____

_____ (Signature of Notary)   (Seal/Stamp of Notary)
Notary Public — State of Washington
My Appointment Expires: _____

- Certificate of acknowledgment for a person signing as a
  representative (e.g. attorney in fact, corporate officer, etc.)
  — wording must be substantially as follows:

State of Washington   )
County of _____)

I certify that I know or have satisfactory evidence that _____
(name of person) is the person who appeared before me, and said
person acknowledged that he/she signed this instrument, on oath stated
that he/she was authorized to execute the instrument and acknowledged
it as the _____ (type of authority, e.g., attorney in fact, officer,
etc.) of _____ (name of party or entity on behalf of whom the
instrument was executed) to be the free and voluntary act of such party
for the uses and purposes mentioned in the instrument.
Dated: _____

_____ (Signature of Notary)   (Seal/Stamp of Notary)
Notary Public — State of Washington
My Appointment Expires: _____

Identification of Acknowledger. In executing an
acknowledgment, the Notary must identify the signer through
personal knowledge or another form of satisfactory evidence (RCW
42.44.080). (See "Identifying Document Signers," pages 38-39.)

Witnessing Signature Not Required. For an acknowledgment,
the document does not have to be signed in the Notary's
presence. As long as the signer appears before the Notary at the
time of notarization to acknowledge having signed, the Notary
may execute the acknowledgment. The document could have
been signed an hour before, a week before, a year before, etc.
— as long as the signer appears before the Notary with the
signed document at the time of notarization to admit that the
signature is his or her own (RCW 42.44.080).

Terminology. In discussing the notarial act of
acknowledgment, it is important to use the proper terminology.
A Notary takes or executes an acknowledgment, while a
document signer makes or gives an acknowledgment.

Who May Take Acknowledgments. Besides Notaries, the
following people may take acknowledgments in Washington
(RCW 64.08.010 and 64.08.090):

- A justice, deputy or clerk of the Supreme Court

- A judge or clerk of a court of appeals

- A judge, court commissioner or clerk of a superior court

- A county auditor or deputy county auditor

- A qualified U.S. commissioner appointed by any district
  court of the United States for the state of Washington

- Certain officers of correctional institutions, provided that
  notarial acts are only performed for officers, employees and
  residents of the particular institution

Outside of Washington, but inside the United States and its jurisdictions, acknowledgments may be executed by (RCW 42.44.130 and 64.08.020):

- A Notary in other U.S. states and jurisdictions.

- A judge, clerk or deputy clerk of a court.

- Any other person authorized in that jurisdiction.

Acknowledgments may be executed under federal authority by (RCW 42.44.130):

- A judge, clerk or deputy clerk of a court.

- A commissioned officer on active duty with the U.S. Armed Forces.

- An officer of the foreign service or a consular officer of the United States.

- Any other person authorized by U.S. federal or foreign law.

Outside of the United States and its jurisdictions, acknowledgments may be executed under foreign authority by (RCW 42.44.130 and 64.08.040):

- A Notary of that jurisdiction.

- A judge, clerk or deputy clerk of a court.

- Any other person authorized in that jurisdiction.

Certified Copies

Purpose. Washington Notaries have authority to certify (or attest) that a copy of an original document is a complete and true reproduction of the document that was copied. The Notary should not certify copies of documents that are either public records or publicly recordable (RCW 42.44.010).

Procedure. The custodian of the document must present the document to the Notary and request a certified copy. A certified copy does not have to be made from an original document. A photocopy may serve as the original as long as it is so described (e.g., a copy of a University of Washington degree).

A common request is to certify a copy of a college diploma. Since only one such document exists, most people do not want to risk parting with the original when proof of their graduate status is requested by a prospective employer or school.

Precautions. Though certification of a transcription or hand-rendered copy is permitted under Washington law, the NNA strongly recommends that Notaries only certify photocopies in order to avert the likelihood that something may be inadvertently omitted or mistranscribed in a handmade copy. Also, to minimize fraud, the Notary should make, or supervise the making of, the photocopy. Regardless, the Notary should carefully compare the copy to the original, word for word, to ensure that it is complete and identical (RCW 42.44.080).

Copy Certification of Vital Records. Washington Notaries should not certify copies of birth and death certificates, marriage licenses, divorce decrees or any other vital records. A Notary's "certification" of such a copy may lend credibility to what is actually a counterfeit or altered document. Only officials in a bureau of vital statistics or other public-record office may certify originals or copies of such certificates and documents. (See "Bureaus of Vital Statistics," pages 109–112.)

Certificate for Certified Copy. Washington statute provides the following short-form certificate wording for certifying a copy of a document (RCW 42.44.100):

State of Washington   )
County of _____)

I certify that this is a true and correct copy of a document in the possession of _____ (name of person presenting document) as of this date.
Dated: _____

_____ (Signature of Notary)   (Seal/Stamp of Notary)
Notary Public — State of Washington
My Appointment Expires: _____

Depositions

Purpose. Although Washington law permits any Notary to take depositions — meaning, to transcribe the words spoken aloud by a deposition signer — this duty is most often executed by Notaries who are trained and certified shorthand reporters, also known as court reporters (RCW 5.28.010).

A deposition is a signed transcript of the signer's oral statements taken down for use in a judicial proceeding. The deposition signer is called the deponent.

With a deposition, both sides in a lawsuit or court case have the opportunity to question the deponent. The questions and answers are transcribed into a written statement, then signed and sworn to before an oath-administering official.

Wording for Deposition Oath (Affirmation). Washington statutes prescribe the following wording to administer to a deponent (RCW 5.28.020, 5.28.040 and 5.28.050):

> You do solemnly swear (affirm) that the evidence you shall give in the issue (or matter) now pending between _____ and _____ shall be the truth, the whole truth, and nothing but the truth, so help you God.

If the oath or affirmation is to be administered to a person other than a witness giving testimony, the wording may be (RCW 5.28.020):

> You do solemnly swear (affirm) you will true answers make to such questions as you may be asked.

Oaths and Affirmations

Purpose. An oath is a solemn, spoken pledge to a Supreme Being. An affirmation is a solemn, spoken pledge on one's own personal honor, with no reference to a Supreme Being. Both are usually a promise or pledge of truthfulness or fidelity and have the same legal effect. In taking an oath or affirmation in an official proceeding, a person may be subject to criminal penalties for perjury should he or she fail to be truthful.

An oath or affirmation can be a full-fledged notarial act in its own right, as when administering an oath of office to a public official (swearing in a public official), or it can be part of the process of notarizing a document (e.g., executing a jurat or swearing in a credible identifying witness).

A person who objects to taking an oath — pledging to a Supreme Being — may instead be given an affirmation, which does not refer to a Supreme Being.

Power to Administer. Washington Notaries and certain other officers are authorized to administer oaths and affirmations (RCW 42.44.010).

Corporate Oaths Prohibited. A person may not take an oath or affirmation on behalf of a legal entity such as a corporation, partnership or other artificial signer. An oath or affirmation, as required by a verification or jurat, is a strictly personal commitment of conscience.

However, notarial certificates may direct Notaries to administer an oath to a corporate signer to compel the person to be truthful about having the authority to sign. In such instances, it is the individual, not the entity, taking the oath.

Wording for Oath (Affirmation). If law does not dictate otherwise, a Washington Notary may use the following or similar words in administering an oath (or affirmation):

• Oath (affirmation) for an affiant signing an affidavit or a deponent signing a deposition:

Do you solemnly swear that the statements in this document are true to the best of your knowledge and belief, so help you God?

(Do you solemnly affirm that the statements in this document are true to the best of your knowledge and belief?)

• Oath (affirmation) for a credible identifying witness identifying a document signer who is in the Notary's presence:

Do you solemnly swear that you personally know this signer truly holds the identity he (or she) claims, so help you God?

(Do you solemnly affirm that you personally know this signer truly holds the identity he [or she] claims?)

Response Required. The oath or affirmation wording must be spoken aloud. The person taking the oath or affirmation must answer affirmatively with "I do," "Yes" or the like. A nod, grunt or other nonverbal reply is not a sufficient response. If a person is unable to speak, the Notary may rely upon written notes to communicate.

Ceremony and Gestures. To stress the importance of truthfulness to the oath-taker or affirmant, the Notary is encouraged to lend a sense of ceremony and formality to the oath or affirmation. During the administration of an oath or affirmation, the Notary and document signer traditionally raise their right hands, though this is not a legal requirement. Notaries generally have discretion to use words and gestures they feel will most compellingly appeal to the conscience of the oath-taker or affirmant.

Verification Upon Oath or Affirmation

Jurat Typically Part of Verification. In notarizing affidavits, depositions and other forms of written verification requiring an oath or affirmation by the signer, the Notary typically executes a jurat (RCW 42.44.010 and 42.44.080).

Purpose. While the purpose of an acknowledgment is to positively identify a document signer, the purpose of a verification with jurat is to compel truthfulness by appealing to the signer's conscience and fear of criminal penalties for perjury. In executing a jurat, a Notary certifies that (42.44.080):

- The signer personally appeared before the Notary at the time of notarization on the date and in the county indicated (notarization based upon a telephone call or on familiarity with a signature is not acceptable).

- The signer was positively identified by the Notary.

- The person making the verification signed the document in the Notary's presence.

- The Notary administered an oath or affirmation to the signer.

Certificate. Certificate wording for a verification upon oath or affirmation is typically jurat wording. Washington law prescribes the following wording (RCW 42.44.100):

State of Washington   )
County of _____)

Signed and sworn to (or affirmed) before me on _____ (date) by
_____ (name of person making statement).

_____ (Signature of Notary)   (Seal/Stamp of Notary)
Notary Public — State of Washington
My Appointment Expires: _____

Identification. When executing a verification upon oath or affirmation, the Notary must positively identify each signer (RCW 42.44.080).

Wording for Jurat Oath (Affirmation). If not otherwise prescribed by law, a Washington Notary may use the following or similar wording to administer an oath or affirmation in conjunction with a jurat:

Do you solemnly swear that the statements in this document are true to the best of your knowledge and belief, so help you God?

(Do you solemnly affirm that the statements in this document are true to the best of your knowledge and belief?)

Witnessing or Attesting a Signature

Purpose. The act of witnessing (or attesting) a signature is similar to a jurat, except that it does not require the signer to take an oath or affirmation. It is used when establishing that the signing date is of major importance.

In witnessing or attesting a signature, the Notary certifies that (RCW 42.44.080):

- The signer personally appeared before the Notary on the date and in the county indicated on the notarial certificate.

- The signer was positively identified by personal knowledge or satisfactory evidence.

- The signer signed the document in the presence of the Notary.

Certificate. A Notary may use the following short-form certificate for witnessing or attesting a signature (RCW 42.44.100):

State of Washington   )
County of _____)

Signed or attested before me on _____ (date) by _____
(name of person appearing).

_____ (Signature of Notary)   (Seal/Stamp of Notary)
Notary Public — State of Washington
My Appointment Expires: _____

Proof of Acknowledgment by Subscribing Witness

Purpose. In executing a proof of acknowledgment by
subscribing witness (also called a proof of execution by a
subscribing witness), a Notary certifies that the signature of a
person who does not appear before the Notary — the principal
signer — is genuine and freely made based upon the sworn
testimony of another person who does appear — the
subscribing witness.

There is no provision in Washington's Notary law that
recognizes a proof of execution as an official notarial act. State
officials say that Notaries may execute these proofs but should
proceed with caution because of the potential for fraud.

In Lieu of Acknowledgment. On recordable real estate
documents, a proof of execution is typically regarded as an
acceptable substitute for an acknowledgment. The signer should
check with his or her real estate professional to see if this is
appropriate in a specific instance.

Subscribing Witness. A subscribing witness is a person who
watches a principal sign a document (or who personally takes
the principal's acknowledgment) and then subscribes (signs) his
or her own name on the document at the principal's request.
This witness brings that document to a Notary on the principal's
behalf and takes an oath or affirmation from the Notary stating
that the principal willingly signed (or acknowledged signing) the
document and requested that the witness also bring the
document to the Notary.

The ideal subscribing witness personally knows the Notary
and the principal signer and has no personal beneficial or
financial interest in the document or transaction. It would be
foolish of the Notary, for example, to rely upon the word of
a subscribing witness presenting for notarization a power of
attorney that names that very witness as attorney in fact.

<u>Oath (or affirmation) for Subscribing Witness</u>. An acceptable oath or affirmation for the subscribing witness might be:

> Do you solemnly swear that you saw (name of the document signer) sign his/her name to this document and that he/she acknowledged to you having executed it for the purposes therein stated, so help you God?
>
> (Do you solemnly affirm that you saw [name of the document signer] sign his/her name to this document and that he/she acknowledged to you having executed it for the purposes therein stated?)

The subscribing witness then signs the Notary's journal, if one is kept, and the Notary completes a proof of execution by subscribing witness certificate, often called a witness jurat.

<u>Identifying Subscribing Witness</u>. Because of the high potential for fraud with this type of notarization, it is recommended that the subscribing witness be personally known to the Notary. Less preferred is identification of the subscribing witness through satisfactory evidence — identification cards or a credible witness.

<u>Certificate</u>. If no wording is provided, the National Notary Association recommends the following certificate wording for a proof of acknowledgment by a subscribing witness:

> State of Washington   )
> County of _____)
>
> On _____ (date), before me, the undersigned, a Notary Public for the state, personally appeared _____ (subscribing witness's name), personally known to me (or proved to me on the basis of _____ [identification method]), to be the person whose name is subscribed to the within instrument, as a witness thereto, who, being by me duly sworn, deposed and said that he/she was present and saw _____ (name of principal), the same person described in and whose name is subscribed to the within and annexed instrument in his/her authorized capacity(ies) as a party thereto, execute the same, and that said affiant subscribed his/her name to the within instrument as a witness at the request of _____ (name of principal).
>
> _____ (Signature of Notary)   (Seal/Stamp of Notary)
> Notary Public — State of Washington
> My Appointment Expires: _____

Certification of an Event or Act

<u>Purpose</u>. Washington Notaries have the authority to certify that an event has occurred or an act has been performed. The

Notary must determine the occurrence or performance, whether from personal knowledge or from satisfactory evidence based upon the oath or affirmation of a credible witness personally known to the Notary (RCW 42.44.080).

Document Required. Certification of an event or act should only be used in conjunction with an attached document (in which the event or act is described). Since Notaries should be impartial, it is recommended that they not certify events or acts involving themselves (e.g., the Notary mailing a check) — this would be similar to a Notary notarizing his or her own signature (RCW 42.44.100).

Procedures. There are few official guidelines about how to perform this type of notarization, but the National Notary Association recommends the following:

- Notaries should not use this type of notarization to endorse any commercial products, services or contests. Endorsements or testimonials by Notaries are strictly prohibited by Washington law (WAC 308-30-160).

- Notaries should only certify events or acts that do not require value judgments on the Notary's part. For example, this type of notarization might be used to certify that someone has mailed a package on a certain date. It should not be used to certify that someone is a person of "good character."

Certificate. Washington statutes prescribe the following short-form certificate (RCW 42.44.100):

> State of Washington   )
> County of _____)
>
> I certify that the event or act described in this document has occurred or been performed.
>
> _____ (Signature of Notary)   (Seal/Stamp of Notary)
> Notary Public — State of Washington
> My Appointment Expires: _____

Protests

Purpose. In rare instances, Washington Notaries may be asked to protest a negotiable instrument for nonpayment.

A protest is a written statement by a Notary or other authorized officer verifying that payment was not received on an instrument such as a bank draft. Failure to pay is called dishonor. Before issuing a certificate of protest, the Notary must present the bank draft or other instrument to the person, firm or institution obliged to pay, a procedure called presentment (RCW 62A.3-501 to 62A.3-503 and 62A.3-505).

Antiquated Act. In the 19th century, protests were common notarial acts in the United States, but they are rarely performed today because of the advent of modern electronic communications and resulting changes in our banking and financial systems. Modern Notaries most often encounter protests in the context of international commerce.

Special Knowledge Required. Notarial acts of protest are complicated and varied, requiring a special knowledge of financial and legal terminology. Only Notaries who have this special knowledge, or who are acting under the supervision of an experienced bank officer or an attorney familiar with the Uniform Commercial Code, should attempt a protest.

Certificate. Washington law prescribes the following wording for execution of a notice of dishonor. The notice of dishonor should be sent by mail to the drawer at the drawer's last known address, and the notice should be in substantially the following form (RCW 62A.3-520 and 62A.3-522):

NOTICE OF DISHONOR OF CHECK

A check drawn by you and made payable by you to _____ in the amount of _____ has not been accepted for payment by _____, which is the drawee bank designated on your check. This check is dated _____, and it is numbered, No._____.

You are CAUTIONED that unless you pay the amount of this check within fifteen days after the date this letter is postmarked, you may very well have to pay the following additional amounts:

(1) Costs of collecting the amount of the check, including an attorney's fee which will be set by the court;

(2) Interest on the amount of the check which shall accrue at the rate of twelve percent per annum from the date of dishonor; and

(3) Three hundred dollars or three times the face amount of the check, whichever is less, by award of the court.

You are also CAUTIONED that law enforcement agencies may be provided with a copy of this notice of dishonor and the check drawn by you for the possibility of proceeding with criminal charges if you

> do not pay the amount of this check within fifteen days after the date this letter is postmarked.
>
> You are advised to make your payment to _____ at the following address:_____

In addition to sending a notice of dishonor to the drawer of the check under RCW 62A.3-520, the holder of the check should execute an affidavit certifying service of the notice by mail. The affidavit of service by mail must be attached to a copy of the notice of dishonor and must be substantially in the following form:

AFFIDAVIT OF SERVICE BY MAIL

I, _____, hereby certify that on the _____ day of _____ (month), ____ (year), a copy of the foregoing Notice was served on _____ by mailing via the United States Postal Service, postage prepaid, at _____, Washington.
Dated: _____
_____ (Signature)

The holder must retain the affidavit with the check, but must also file a copy of the affidavit with the clerk of the court in which an action on the check is commenced (RCW 62A.3-522).

PRACTICES AND PROCEDURES

Identifying Document Signers

Three Methods of Identification. Washington law requires the Notary to positively identify the signer for all notarial acts except for copy certifications and protests. The following three methods of identification are acceptable (RCW 42.44.080 and WAC 308-30-155):

- The Notary's personal knowledge of the signer's identity (see "Personal Knowledge of Identity," page 39)

- Reliable, current identification documents or ID cards (see "Identification Documents [ID Cards]," pages 39-40)

- The oath or affirmation of a personally known credible identifying witness (See "Credible Identifying Witness," pages 40-41.)

Identification for Other Notarial Acts. While the law does not specify identification standards for copy certification and protests, the prudent and conscientious Notary will apply the above

identification standards to identify all persons requesting
a notarial act.

Proof of Representative Capacity. The Notary is encouraged to
ask for proof of a person's authority to sign in a representative
capacity. However, an acknowledgment certificate indicating that
the signer took an oath or affirmation declaring that he or she
had authority to sign is generally regarded as sufficient proof
of authority (RCW 42.44.010).

Personal Knowledge of Identity
Definition. The safest and most reliable method of identifying
a document signer is for the Notary to depend upon his or her
own personal knowledge of the signer's identity. Personal
knowledge means familiarity with an individual resulting from
interactions with that person over a period of time sufficient to
eliminate every reasonable doubt that the person has the identity
claimed (RCW 42.44.080).

Washington law does not specify how long a Notary must be
acquainted with an individual before personal knowledge of
identity may be claimed. The Notary's common sense must prevail.
In general, the longer the Notary is acquainted with a person, and
the more interactions the Notary has had with that person, the
more likely the individual is personally known.

For instance, the Notary might safely regard a friend since
childhood as personally known, but would be foolish to consider a
person met briefly for the first time as such upon a second meeting.
Whenever the Notary has a reasonable doubt about a signer's
identity, that individual should not be considered personally
known, and the identification should be made through either a
credible identifying witness or reliable identification documents.

Identification Documents (ID Cards)
Acceptable Identification Documents. Washington requires
that an identifying document or card relied upon by a Notary to
identify a stranger be current, be issued by a federal or a state
governmental agency and contain a photograph, physical
description and signature of the bearer (RCW 42.44.080 and
WAC 308-30-155).

Multiple Identification. Identification documents that meet

the criteria described above are sufficient to identify a signer. However, a Notary may ask for additional identification, especially if the Notary suspects fraud. (See "Fraudulent Identification" below.)

Fraudulent Identification. Identification documents are the least secure of the three methods of identifying a document signer, because phony ID cards are common. The Notary should scrutinize each card for evidence of tampering or counterfeiting, or for evidence that it is a genuine card issued to an impostor.

Some clues that an ID card may have been fraudulently tampered with include: mismatched type styles, a photograph raised from the surface, a signature that does not match the signature on the document, unauthorized lamination of the card and smudges, erasures, smears or discolorations.

One of the following may lead you to believe that an act of ID counterfeiting has occurred: misspelled words, inappropriate patterns and textures, a new-looking card with an old date of issuance and two cards with exactly the same photograph.

Some possible indications that a card may have been issued to an impostor include: the card's birth date or address is unknown to the bearer, all of the ID cards seem brand new and the bearer is unwilling to leave a thumbprint in the journal. Such a print is not a requirement of law but is requested by some Notaries as protection against forgeries and lawsuits. Refusal to leave a thumbprint is not in and of itself grounds to deny a notarization.

Credible Identifying Witness

Purpose. When a document signer is not personally known to the Notary and is not able to present reliable ID cards, that signer may be identified on the oath (or affirmation) of a credible identifying witness (or credible witness) (RCW 42.44.080 and WAC 308-30-155).

Qualifications. A credible identifying witness must be personally known to the Notary, as required by Washington law. The document signer, as required by the Washington Administrative Code, must be personally known to the credible identifying witness. (See "Personal Knowledge of Identity," page 39.) There should be a chain of personal knowledge linking the Notary to the credible identifying witness to the signer. In a sense, a credible identifying witness is a walking, talking ID card (RCW 42.44.080 and WAC 308-30-155).

A reliable credible identifying witness should have a reputation for honesty. The witness should be a capable individual who would not be tricked, cajoled, bullied or otherwise influenced into identifying someone he or she does not really know. And the witness, ideally, should have no personal, beneficial or financial interest in the transaction requiring a notarial act.

Oath (Affirmation) for Credible Identifying Witness. An oath or affirmation must be administered to the credible identifying witness by the Notary to compel truthfulness.

If not otherwise prescribed by law, a Washington Notary may use the following or similar wording to administer an oath (or affirmation) to a credible identifying witness:

> Do you solemnly swear that you know the signer truly holds the identity he (or she) claims, so help you God?

> (Do you solemnly affirm that you know the signer truly holds the identity he [or she] claims?)

Journal Entry. If the Notary keeps a journal, the credible identifying witness's name and residence address should be recorded. Prudent Notaries will also ask the witness to sign the journal.

Not a Subscribing Witness. Do not confuse a credible identifying witness with a subscribing witness. A credible identifying witness vouches for the identity of a signer who appears before the Notary. A subscribing witness vouches for the genuineness of the signature of a signer who does not appear before the Notary. (See "Proof of Acknowledgment by Subscribing Witness," pages 34-35.)

Journal of Notarial Acts and Notarial Records

Recommendation. The National Notary Association strongly recommends that every Notary keep a detailed, accurate and sequential journal of notarial acts even though it is not required by Washington law.

Prudent Notaries keep detailed and accurate journals of their notarial acts for many reasons:

- Keeping records is a businesslike practice that every conscientious businessperson and public official should follow. Not keeping records of important transactions, whether public or private, is risky.

- A Notary's record book protects the public's rights to valuable property and due process by providing proof in the event a document is lost or altered, or if a transaction is later challenged.

- In the event of a lawsuit alleging that the Notary's negligence or misconduct financially harmed a plaintiff, a detailed journal can protect the Notary by showing that the Notary used reasonable care when performing all parts of the notarial act.

- Since these lawsuits typically take place three to six years after the alleged act occurs, a journal could aid the Notary's memory about the details of a particular notarization.

- Requiring each document signer to leave a signature and a thumbprint in the Notary's journal deters forgeries and provides strong evidence for a conviction should a forgery occur.

Journal Entries. For each notarization, the following vital information should be recorded:

- The date, time of day and type of notarization (e.g., jurat or acknowledgment)

- The date and type of document notarized (e.g., deed of trust or affidavit of support)

- The printed name, address and the signature of each person whose signature is notarized, the signature of any credible or subscribing witness and the signature of any witnesses to a signature by mark

- A statement as to how each signer was identified (If by personal knowledge, the journal entry should read "Personal Knowledge." If by satisfactory evidence, the journal entry should contain either: a description of the ID card accepted, including the type of ID, the government agency issuing the ID, the serial or identifying number and the date of issuance or expiration; or the signature of each credible identifying witness.) (See "Credible Identifying Witness," pages 40-41.)

- The fee charged for the notarial service if any

Additional Entries. Notaries may include additional information in their journals that is pertinent to a given notarization. For example, many Notaries enter the telephone number of all of the other signers and witnesses, as well as the address where the notarization was performed if not at the Notary's office. A description of the document signer's demeanor (e.g., "The signer appeared very nervous") or notations about the identity of other persons who were present for the notarization may also be pertinent.

One important entry to include is the signer's representative capacity — whether the signer is acting as attorney in fact, trustee, guardian, corporate officer or in another capacity — if not signing on his or her own behalf.

Increasingly, Notaries are asking document signers to leave a thumbprint in the journal as a deterrent to fraud, since no forger wants to leave a print behind as evidence of an attempted crime.

Since a journal record of a notarial act is not required by law, refusal to leave a signature or fingerprint in the journal is not in and of itself sufficient grounds for the Notary to refuse to honor an otherwise lawful and reasonable request for a notarization.

Journal-Entry Copies. A Notary's official journal is a public record. Accordingly, if any person submits a written request specifying the month and year of a particular notarization, the type of document and the names of the signers, the Notary may provide that person with a photocopy of the particular entry in the journal — but of no other entries. Adjacent entries should be covered by a sheet of blank paper before the photocopy is made.

The National Notary Association discourages "fishing expeditions" through the Notary journal by persons who are not able to be specific about the entry they are seeking.

Never Surrender Journal. Notaries should never surrender control of their journals to anyone, unless subpoenaed by a court order. Even when an employer has paid for the Notary's journal, it goes with the Notary upon termination of employment. No one but the Notary can lawfully possess and use this official tool of office.

Notarial Certificate

Requirement. In notarizing any document, a Notary must complete a notarial certificate. The certificate is wording that indicates exactly what the Notary has certified. The notarial certificate may be typed or printed on the document itself or on an attachment (RCW 42.44.090).

The certificate should contain (RCW 42.44.090 and WAC 308-30-120):

- A venue, which indicates where the notarization is being performed. "State of Washington, County of _____" is the typical venue wording, with the appropriate county inserted in the blank. The letters "SS." or "SCT." sometimes appear after the venue and abbreviate the Latin word *scilicet*, meaning "in particular" or "namely."

- A statement of particulars that indicates what the notarization has certified. An acknowledgment certificate would include such wording as: "This instrument was acknowledged before me on _____ (date) by _____ (name of signer)." A jurat certificate would include such wording as: "Signed and sworn to (or affirmed) before me on _____ (date) by _____ (name of signer)."

- A testimonium clause, which may be optional if the date is included in the statement of particulars: "Witness my hand and official seal, this _____ day of _____ (month), _____ (year)." In this phrase, the Notary formally attests to the truthfulness of the preceding facts in the certificate. "Hand" means signature.

- The official signature of the Notary, exactly as the name appears on the Notary's appointment certificate and his or her official seal/stamp.

- The official seal or stamp of the Notary. Many certificates contain the letters "L.S." which indicates where the Notary's seal is to be placed. The letters abbreviate the Latin term *locus sigilli,* meaning "location of the seal." An inking stamp should be placed near but not over the letters, so that wording imprinted by the stamp will not be obscured. An embossing seal may be affixed over the letters.

Loose Certificates. When appropriate certificate wording is not preprinted on the document for the Notary to fill out, a loose certificate may be attached. Normally, this form is stapled to the document's left margin on the signature page. Only one side of the certificate should be stapled so that it can be lifted in order to view the document beneath it.

To prevent a loose certificate from being removed and fraudulently placed on another document, there are precautions a Notary can take. For instance, the Notary can write a brief description of the document on the certificate: "This certificate is attached to a _____ (title or type of document), dated _____, of _____ (number) pages, also signed by _____ (name[s] of other signer[s])."

While fraud-deterrent steps such as this one can make it much more difficult for a loose certificate to be removed and misused, there is no absolute protection against removal and misuse. However, Notaries must ensure that, while a certificate remains in their control, it is attached only to its intended document. A Notary must never give or mail a signed and stamped notarial certificate to another person and trust that person to attach it to a particular document. This would be an indefensible action in civil court.

Must Be Page-Size. No paper attachments bearing Notary certificate wording may be stapled, taped or glued to the pages of a document that will be recorded by county auditors in Washington.

If appropriate notarial certificate wording (e.g., acknowledgment or jurat) is not printed or typed on the document itself, the certificate only may be attached if it is on a sheet exactly the same size as the document's other pages and fastened in the same manner as the other pages.

Documents with notarial forms that are less than a full page in size will be rejected by the county auditor. In addition, no document page or notarial certificate may be larger than 8½ by 14 inches (RCW 65.04.045).

Must Have One-Inch Margin. Any document presented for recording in Washington must have a one-inch margin on the top, bottom and sides of all pages, except for the first page, which must have a top margin of at least three inches. Thus, any Notary certificate attached to a recordable document must not only be page-sized but must also have a top, bottom and side margin of at least one inch (RCW 65.04.045).

County auditors will permit a Notary's seal, incidental writing or a minor portion of a signature to protrude into the margin. Such instances will not affect a document's recording (RCW 65.04.045).

Type Not Less Than Eight Points. No page or Notary certificate may contain printing smaller than 8 points (RCW 65.04.045).

Documents Not Recorded in Washington. Pages and Notary certificates on documents that will not be recorded in Washington by a county auditor may not need to adhere to specified format requirements. However, to avoid an unintentional mistake, the National Notary Association encourages Washington Notaries to consistently use certificates that adhere to this format regardless of where the signer intends to have the document recorded.

Selecting Certificates. Washington law specifically prohibits Notaries from selecting notarial certificates for any transaction. However, this does not prevent a Notary who is duly licensed and qualified in a particular field from giving advice relating to matters in that specific field (WAC 308-30-090).

To be safe, if a document is presented to a Notary without certificate wording, and the signer cannot indicate what type of notarization (e.g., acknowledgment or verification) is appropriate, the NNA recommends that the signer be asked to find out what type of notarization and certificate are needed. Usually the agency that issued or will be accepting the document can provide this information.

Do Not Pre-Sign/Seal Certificates. A Notary should never sign or seal certificates ahead of time or permit other persons to attach loose notarial certificates to documents. Also, the Notary should never send an unattached, signed and sealed loose certificate through the mail, even if asked to do so by a signer who previously appeared before the Notary. These actions may facilitate fraud or forgery, and they could subject the Notary to lawsuits to recover damages resulting from the Notary's neglect or misconduct.

Short Form Certificates. Washington Notaries may use the following short-form certificates for the purposes indicated (RCW 42.44.100):

• Acknowledgment by person signing in an individual capacity:

State of Washington   )
County of _____)

I certify that I know or have satisfactory evidence that (name of person) is the person who appeared before me, and said person acknowledged that he/she signed this instrument and acknowledged it to be his/her free and voluntary act for the uses and purposes mentioned in the instrument.
Dated: _____

_____ (Signature of Notary)   (Seal/Stamp of Notary)
Notary Public — State of Washington
My Appointment Expires: _____

• For an acknowledgment in a representative capacity:

State of Washington   )
County of _____)

I certify that I know or have satisfactory evidence that (name of person) is the person who appeared before me, and said person acknowledged that he/she signed this instrument, on oath stated that he/she was authorized to execute the instrument and acknowledged it as the (type of authority, e.g., officer, trustee, etc.) of (name of party on behalf of whom instrument was executed) to be the free and voluntary act of such party for the uses and purposes mentioned in the instrument.
Dated: _____

_____ (Signature of Notary)   (Seal/Stamp of Notary)
Notary Public — State of Washington
My Appointment Expires: _____

- For a verification upon oath or affirmation:

State of Washington)
County of _____)

Signed and sworn to (or affirmed) before me on _____ (date) by
_____ (name[s] of person[s] making statement).

_____ (Signature of Notary)   (Seal/Stamp of Notary)
Notary Public — State of Washington
My Appointment Expires: _____

- For witnessing or attesting a signature:

State of Washington)
County of _____)

Signed or attested before me on _____ (date) by
_____ (name[s] of person[s]).

_____ (Signature of Notary)   (Seal/Stamp of Notary)
Notary Public — State of Washington
My Appointment Expires: _____

- For certifying or attesting a copy of a document:

State of Washington)
County of _____)

I certify that this is a true and correct copy of a document in the
possession of _____ as of this date.
Dated: _____

_____ (Signature of Notary)   (Seal/Stamp of Notary)
Notary Public — State of Washington
My Appointment Expires: _____

- For certifying the occurrence of an event or the
  performance of an act:

State of Washington)
County of _____)

I certify that the event or act described in this document has occurred
or been performed.
Dated: _____

_____ (Signature of Notary)   (Seal/Stamp of Notary)
Notary Public — State of Washington
My Appointment Expires: _____

<u>False Certificate</u>. A Notary Public who knowingly creates or completes a false notarial certificate may be guilty of a gross misdemeanor (RCW 42.20.050 and 42.44.160).

In addition, a Notary who falsely completes a written instrument — for example, filling in a document's blank spaces — may be guilty of a Class C Felony alleging forgery with intent to deceive or defraud (RCW 9A.60.020).

<u>Illegible Imprint or Writing</u>. The illegibility of any wording, writing, marking or seal or stamp impression on the document or certificate does not necessarily invalidate the notarization (RCW 42.44.110).

<u>Validity of Telegraphic Copies</u>. Any instrument in writing that has been notarized may be transmitted by telegraph. The telegraphic copy shall be considered *prima facie* evidence to have the same validity and effect as if it were an original. The burden of proof shall rest on the party denying the genuineness of the document (RCW 5.52.050).

Notary Seal or Stamp

<u>Embosser or Inking Stamp</u>. As required by law, a Washington Notary must affix an impression of an official seal or inking stamp on the certificate portion of every document notarized. However, a seal or inking stamp is not required in certifying an oath for use in any court in the state of Washington. The impression may not be placed over any signature or wording on a notarial certificate. The stamp must print a photographically reproducible impression in indelible black ink. A hand-drawn seal is not acceptable (RCW 42.44.050, 42.44.090 and WAC 308-30-010).

<u>Format</u>. The inking stamp must be rectangular or circular. If it is rectangular, it must measure a minimum of 1 inch high and 1⅛ inches long. If it is circular, it must measure a minimum of 1⅛ inches in diameter.

The embossing seal must be circular and a minimum of 1⅛ inches in diameter (WAC 308-30-010).

<u>Required Information</u>. The Notary seal or stamp must contain the following elements (RCW 42.44.050 and WAC 308-30-010):

- The surname and at least the initials of the first and middle names of the Notary Public in not less than 8-point type.

- The words "Notary Public" and "State of Washington," printed in not less than 8-point type.

- The Notary's commission expiration date, printed in not less than 8-point type.

Use of Expired Seal Prohibited. Use of a Notary's seal or stamp with an expired date is expressly prohibited by law (WAC 308-30-130).

Use of State Seal Prohibited. Use of the Washington State Seal on the Notary seal or stamp is forbidden (WAC 308-30-010).

Embosser. Many Notaries use an embosser — called a seal in Washington statutes — in addition to the required photographically reproducible stamp, but it must not be affixed over the stamp or over the Notary's signature.
The embosser may be affixed over the letters "L.S." — abbreviating the Latin term *locus sigilli*, meaning "location of the seal" — that appear on many notarial certificates to indicate where the notarial seal should be placed.

Placement of the Seal/Stamp Impression. The Notary's official seal or stamp impression should be placed near (but not over) the Notary's signature on the notarial certificate. If there is no room for a seal or stamp, the Notary may have no choice but to complete and attach a loose certificate that duplicates the notarial wording on the document.

Authorization to Purchase Seal or Stamp. When a Notary application has been approved, the Secretary of State sends the new Notary a Certificate of Appointment, a photocopy of which authorizes purchase of the required Notary seal or stamp (RCW 42.44.050).

Seal/Embosser Manufacturer. A seal or embosser vendor may not provide a person with a Notary seal or embosser without a photocopy of the person's Notary Certificate of Appointment. If a new seal or embosser is required because of a Notary's name change, the vendor must receive a copy of the new certificate showing the change (WAC 308-30-100).

Preprinted Seal Prohibited. The Notary's inking seal or embosser must contain permanently affixed letters and numbers and may not be preprinted, for example, by computer or digital imaging (WAC 308-30-010).

Lost or Stolen Seal or Stamp. If a Notary's seal or stamp is lost or stolen, the Notary must mail or deliver a written notice to the Department of Licensing by certified mail.

The notice must state that the seal or stamp has been lost or stolen, and it must be signed by the Notary. The Notary may then obtain a replacement seal or stamp which must contain some variance from the original seal or stamp. (If only initials were used on the original, for example, include the full name on the replacement seal or stamp.)

If the original seal or stamp is found or recovered after another has been obtained, the original must be surrendered to the Department of Licensing (WAC 308-30-050).

Disposition of the Notary's Seal or Stamp. Upon revocation or resignation of the Notary's appointment, the Notary seal or stamp must be delivered to the Department of Licensing (WAC 308-30-040).

When a Notary resigns the appointment, the Notary seal or stamp must be filed with the Department of Licensing at the same time the Notary files the letter of resignation (WAC 308-30-040).

When an appointment expires after the four-year term, the Notary is not required to submit the seal or stamp to the Department of Licensing. However, the Notary should destroy the seal or stamp as soon as possible to eliminate the chance of fraudulent use.

Should the Notary die during the commission term, the Notary's personal representative should destroy the seal or stamp. Any notarial records (e.g., the journal) should be retained for the amount of time prescribed by the statute of limitations, which is up to six years for written contracts.

Seal/Embosser Sole Property of Notary. The Notary seal and embosser are the exclusive property of the Notary named on them and must not be used by any other person or surrendered to an employer upon termination of the Notary's employment, regardless of who paid for them (RCW 42.44.090).

Fees for Notarial Services

Maximum Fees. Effective November 1, 2006, administrative rule amended Section 308-30-020-19 of the Washington Administrative Code, increasing the fees a Notary may charge. The following maximum fees are now authorized for Washington Notaries (WAC 308-30-020-19):

- Acknowledgments — $10. For taking an acknowledgment, the Notary may charge $10.

- Certified Copies — $10. For certifying a copy, the Notary may charge $10 for each certified copy certificate. For copying any instrument or record, a Notary may charge the actual cost of copying the instrument or record.

- Oaths and Affirmations — $10. For administering an oath or affirmation, the Notary may charge $10 per person.

- Verification Upon Oath or Affirmation — $10. For executing a jurat on an affidavit or other form of verification upon an oath or affirmation, the Notary may charge $10.

- Witnessing or Attesting a Signature — $10. For witnessing or attesting a signature, the Notary may charge $10 per signature.

- Proof of Acknowledgment by Subscribing Witness — $10. Although the fee is not prescribed by law, state officials suggest that a Notary charge the same amount as for the performance of an acknowledgment.

- Certifying an Event or Act — $10. For certifying that an event has occurred or an act has been performed, the Notary may charge $10.

- Protests — $10. For protesting a bill or note, the fee is $10.

Travel Fees. A Washington Notary may charge a fee for travel only if (WAC 308-30-020):

- The Notary and the person requesting the notarial act agree upon the travel fee in advance of the travel.

- The Notary explains to the person requesting the notarial act that the travel fee is in addition to the notarial fee and is not required by law.

Option Not to Charge. Notaries are not required to charge for their notarial services. And they may charge any fee less than the statutory maximum (RCW 42.44.120 and WAC 308-30-020).

Overcharging. Charging more than the prescribed maximum fees is considered "requesting unlawful compensation," a Class C felony (RCW 9A.68.020).

Posting of Fees. A Washington Notary who charges fees for notarial services is required to display in a conspicuous area in his or her place of business, or present to each customer outside the business, a notice of the fees allowed by law to be charged. The notice must be in English and be in at least 10-point type (WAC 308-30-020).

Disqualifying Interest

Impartiality. Notaries are appointed by the state to be impartial, disinterested witnesses whose screening duties help ensure the integrity of important legal and commercial transactions. Lack of impartiality by a Notary throws doubt on the integrity and lawfulness of any transaction. A Notary must never notarize his or her own signature, or notarize in a transaction in which the Notary is named (RCW 42.44.080).

Financial or Beneficial Interest. A Notary should not perform any notarization related to a transaction in which that Notary or the Notary's spouse has a direct financial or beneficial interest. A financial or beneficial interest exists when the Notary or the Notary's spouse is individually named as a principal in a financial transaction or when the Notary receives an advantage, right, privilege, property or fee valued in excess of the lawfully prescribed notarial fee.

With regard to real estate transactions, a Notary is generally considered to have a disqualifying financial or beneficial interest when that Notary or the Notary's spouse is a grantor or grantee; mortgagor or mortgagee; trustor or trustee; lessor or lessee; or a beneficiary in any way of the transaction.

Relatives. The National Notary Association strongly discourages Notaries from notarizing for persons related by blood or marriage because of the likelihood of a financial or beneficial interest.

Refusal of Services

Legal Request for Services. Notaries must honor all lawful and reasonable requests to notarize (RCW 42.20.100).

A person's race, gender, religion, nationality, ethnicity, lifestyle or politics is never legitimate cause for refusing to perform a notarial act. As a public servant, a Notary should treat all people fairly and equally.

Reasonable Care

Responsibility. As public servants, Notaries must act responsibly and exercise reasonable care in the performance of their official duties. If a Notary fails to do so, he or she may be subject to a lawsuit to recover financial damages caused by the Notary's error or omission.

In general, reasonable care is that degree of concern and attentiveness that a person of normal intelligence and responsibility would exhibit. If a Notary can show a judge or jury that he or she did everything expected of a reasonable person, the judge or jury is obligated by law to find the Notary not liable for damages.

Complying with all pertinent laws is the first rule of reasonable care for a Notary. If there are no statutory guidelines in a given instance, the Notary should take all reasonable steps to use common sense and prudence. (See "Steps to Proper Notarization," pages 13-17.)

Blank or Incomplete Documents

Against Common Sense. While Washington law does not specifically address notarizing blank or incomplete documents, this dangerous, unbusinesslike practice is widely discouraged as a breach of common sense, similar to signing a blank check.

A fraudulent document could be readily created above a Notary's certificate on a blank sheet of paper. Also, with documents containing blanks to be filled in after notarization, there is a danger that the information inserted later may be against the signer's wishes.

Employer/Notary Relationship

Notary Accountable to State. Even when an employer has paid for a Notary's commissioning fees, seal, journal and supplies, the Notary's primary allegiance is to the laws of the State of Washington, not to the employer (RCW 42.44.090).

An employer or supervisor might ask a Notary to notarize the signature of a person who is not present. Doing so is against the law, and the Notary may be held civilly and criminally liable. Notaries must always remember that the primary responsibility and financial liability for performing an illegal or improper notarial act belong exclusively to the Notary, although an employer may be penalized for coercing or threatening the Notary.

Unauthorized Practice of Law

Do Not Assist with Legal Matters. A nonattorney Notary may not give legal advice or accept fees for legal advice. As a ministerial officer, a nonattorney Notary is generally not permitted to assist in drafting, preparing, completing or explaining a document or transaction.

The Notary should not fill in blank spaces in the text of a document for other persons, tell others what documents they need or how to draft them or advise others about the legal sufficiency of a document — and especially not for a fee.

A Notary, of course, may fill in the blanks on the notarial certificate. And a Notary, as a private individual, may prepare legal documents to which he or she is personally a party, but the Notary may not then notarize his or her signature on those documents.

Notaries who overstep their authority by advising others on legal matters may be guilty of a gross misdemeanor for the first offense. Each subsequent offense is a Class C Felony (RCW 2.48.170, 2.48.180 and WAC 308-30-090).

Exceptions. Nonattorney Notaries who are specially trained, certified or licensed in a particular field (e.g., real estate, insurance or escrow) may advise others about documents in that field only. In addition, trained paralegals under the supervision of an attorney may advise others about documents in routine legal matters (WAC 308-30-090).

Signature by Mark

Mark Serves as Signature. A person who cannot sign his

or her name because of illiteracy or a physical disability may instead use a mark — an "X," for example — as a signature, as long as there are witnesses to the making of the mark.

Witnesses for Notarization. For a signature by mark to be notarized, there should be two impartial witnesses (in addition to the Notary) to the making of the mark. Both witnesses also should sign the document, and one witness should write out the marker's name beside the mark. It is recommended that a mark also be affixed in the Notary's journal, if kept, and that the witnesses also sign the journal.

Notarization Procedures. Because a properly witnessed mark is regarded as a legal signature, no special procedures or certificates are required. The marker must be positively identified, as with any other signer, and regular notarial certificates may be used.

Notarizing for a Person Who Directs Another to Sign

Persons with a Disability. If a person cannot sign a document because of a physical disability, he or she may direct the Notary to sign on his or her behalf (RCW 42.44.080 and 64.08.100).

Notarization. A Notary may notarize this signature but should take extra care to avoid any problems. The Notary must determine the person's willingness and awareness of the transaction.

In addition, the Notary should positively identify the person through personal knowledge, a credible identifying witness or ID cards.

Certificate. The Notary's acknowledgment certificate must state the Notary's name and place of residence, and that the principal's signature was affixed according to RCW 64.08.100 (RCW 42.44.080 and 64.08.100).

When no notarial wording is provided, the National Notary Association suggests the following wording:

State of Washington)
County of _____)

I certify that I know or have satisfactory evidence that _____
(name of person unable to sign) is the person who appeared before

me and that said person was unable to write his/her name or to make a mark and appears otherwise capable, and that said person orally directed me to write his/her signature on this instrument on his/her behalf under authority of RCW 64.08.100, and acknowledged it to be his/her free and voluntary act for the uses and purposes mentioned in the attached instrument.

Dated: _____

_____ (Signature of Notary)   (Seal/Stamp of Notary)
Notary Public — State of Washington
My Appointment Expires: _____

Journal Entry. The prudent Notary will record the specific circumstances of the notarization in a journal. In addition, the Notary should note that he or she affixed the principal's signature according to RCW 64.08.100.

Marriages

No Authority to Perform. A Washington Notary does not have the authority to perform a marriage ceremony unless the person is also a member of the clergy or an official authorized to solemnize marriages. However, any person may obtain a marriage license by mail, execute it and acknowledge it before a Notary (RCW 26.04.150).

Notarizing for Minors

Under Age 18. Generally, persons must reach the age of majority before they can handle their own legal affairs and sign documents for themselves. In Washington, the age of majority is 18. Normally, parents or court-appointed guardians will sign on a minor's behalf. In certain cases, minors may lawfully sign documents and have their signatures notarized — minors engaged in business transactions or children serving as court witnesses, for example.

Include Age next to Signature. When notarizing for a minor, the Notary should ask the young signer to write his or her age next to the signature on the document and in the journal. This will alert any interested party that the signer is a minor. The Notary is not required to verify the minor's age.

Identification. The method for identifying a minor is the same as that for an adult. However, determining the identity of a minor can be problematic because minors often do not possess acceptable identification documents, such as driver's licenses or passports. If the minor does not have an acceptable ID, then the other methods of identifying signers must be used: either the Notary's personal knowledge of the minor or the oath of a credible identifying witness who can identify the minor. (See "Identifying Document Signers," pages 38-39.)

Authentication

Documents Sent out of State. Documents notarized in Washington and sent out of state may be required to bear proof that the Notary's signature and stamp are genuine and that the Notary had authority to act at the time of notarization. This process of proving the genuineness of an official signature and stamp is called authentication or legalization.

In Washington State, the proof is in the form of an authenticating certificate attached to the notarized document by the Department of Licensing. Washington regulations prescribe that a person needing an authentication certificate contact the Department of Licensing directly (RCW 42.44.180 and WAC 308-30-070).

Authenticating certificates are known by many different names: certificates of official character, certificates of authority, certificates of capacity and flags.

The fee for an authenticating certificate is $15 per document (by check, payable to "Washington State Treasurer"). The certificate may be obtained by mail by writing to: Department of Licensing, Notary Public Section, P.O. Box 9048, Olympia, WA 98507-9048. Additional information is available by calling (360) 664-1550.

The original notarized document must be forwarded with the written request, the Notary's name, the Notary's commission expiration date and the fee. It is not the Notary's responsibility to pick up or pay for the certificate of authority.

Authenticating certificates are also available from the Washington Secretary of State's Office. More information is available at www.secstate.wa.gov/apostilles.

Documents Sent Out of Country. If a notarized document will be sent outside the United States, a chain-authentication process may be necessary, and additional certificates of authority may have to be obtained from the U.S. Department of State and different ministries of a given foreign nation, here and abroad. This chain-certification process can be time-consuming and expensive. Contact the Department of Licensing at (360) 664-1550 for more information.

Apostilles and the Hague Convention. Fortunately, more than 90 nations, including the United States, subscribe to a treaty under the auspices of the Hague Conference that simplifies authentication of notarized documents exchanged between any of these nations. The official name of this treaty, adopted by the Conference on October 5, 1961, is the *Hague Convention Abolishing the Requirement of Legalization for Foreign Public Documents*. (For a list of the subscribing countries, see "Hague Convention Nations," pages 113-115.)

Under the Hague Convention, only one authenticating certificate called an *apostille* is necessary to ensure acceptance of a Notary's signature and seal or stamp in these subscribing countries. (*Apostille* means "notation" in French.) In Washington, *apostilles* are issued by the Department of Licensing. The fees and procedures are the same as for obtaining an ordinary authenticating certificate, except that the country for which the document is destined should also be specified in the written request (RCW 42.44.180 and WAC 308-30-070).

Foreign Languages

Non-English Advertising. A nonattorney Notary advertising notarial services in a foreign language must take steps to guard against misinterpretation of his or her function as a Notary. Notaries are encouraged to include in any such foreign language advertisement the following information in English and the foreign language:

- The statement *"I am not licensed to practice law in the State of Washington, and I am not permitted to give legal advice on immigration or other legal matters or accept fees for legal advice."*

- The statutory fees a Notary is allowed to charge

Notaries are encouraged to include the above information when advertising with signs and all other forms of written communication (e.g., business cards, yellow page ads, e-mails).

Furthermore, literal translation of "Notary Public" into Spanish (*Notario Publico* or *Notaria Publica*) or into any equivalent non-English term should be avoided in order to prevent any misunderstanding by non-English speakers.

Foreign-Language Documents. Ideally, documents in foreign languages should be referred to Washington Notaries who read and write those languages. If not available in the general public, bilingual Notaries may often be found in foreign consulates.

Washington law does not directly address notarizing documents written in a language the Notary cannot read. Although notarizing such documents is not expressly prohibited, there are difficulties and dangers in notarizing any document the Notary cannot understand. The foremost danger is that the document may have been misrepresented to the Notary. The Notary cannot know if the document is false or endorses or promotes a product using the Notary seal and may unknowingly perform an illegal act or facilitate fraud by notarizing it.

If a Notary chooses to notarize a document that he or she cannot read, then the notarial certificate should be either in English or in a language the Notary can read.

Foreign-Language Signers. There should always be direct communication between the Notary and document signer — whether in English or any other language. The Notary should never rely upon an intermediary or interpreter to be assured that a signer is willing to execute a document and understands the significance of the transaction, since this third party may have a motive for misrepresenting the circumstances to the Notary and/or the signer.

Immigration

Do Not Give Advice. Nonattorney Notaries may never advise others on the subject of immigration or help others prepare immigration documents — and especially not for a fee. Notaries who offer immigration advice to others may be prosecuted for the unauthorized practice of law (WAC 308-30-090).

Documents. Affidavits are the forms issued or accepted by U.S. Citizenship and Immigration Services (USCIS) that most often require notarization, with the Affidavit of Support

(I-134/I-864) being perhaps the most common. Non-USCIS-issued documents are often notarized and submitted in support of an immigration or naturalization petition. These might include translator's declarations, statements from employers and banks and affidavits of relationship.

If there appears to be no room for the Notary seal or stamp on a USCIS-issued document, federal officials advise that it may be affixed over standard preprinted clauses or sections.

Copies of Naturalization Certificates Prohibited. The law imposes harsh penalties for printing or photographing a certificate of naturalization without lawful authority. The NNA recommends that a Notary only certify a copy of a certificate of naturalization if written directions are provided by a U.S. immigration authority.

Military-Personnel Notarizations

May Notarize Worldwide. Certain U.S. military personnel may notarize for other military personnel and their dependents anywhere in the world. Under federal statutory authority, the following persons are authorized to act as Notaries:

- Civilian attorneys employed as legal-assistance attorneys and licensed to practice law in the United States

- Judge advocates on active duty or training as reservists on inactive duty

- All adjutants, assistant adjutants, acting adjutants and personnel adjutants

- Enlisted paralegals, personnel rank of E-4 or higher, on active duty or training on inactive duty

- Active duty personnel who are commissioned officers or senior noncommissioned officers (rank E-7 or higher) who are stationed at a Geographically Separated Unit (GSU) or location where no authorized Notary official is available and who are appointed in writing by the unit's servicing general court-martial convening authority

Certificate. When signing documents in their official capacity, military-officer Notaries must specify the date and location of the

WASHINGTON NOTARY LAW PRIMER

notarization, list their title and office, and use a raised seal or inked stamp citing Title 10 U.S.C. 1044a (U.S. Code, Title 10, Sections 936, 1044a).

Authentication. Authentication of a military-officer notarization certificate is not required.

Wills

Do Not Offer Advice. People often attempt to draw up wills on their own without benefit of legal counsel and then bring these homemade testaments to a Notary to have them "legalized," expecting the Notary to know how to proceed. In advising or assisting such persons, the Notary risks prosecution for the unauthorized practice of law. The Notary's ill-informed advice might do considerable damage to the affairs of the signer and subject the Notary to a lawsuit to recover losses.

Wills are highly sensitive documents whose format is dictated by strict laws. The slightest deviation from these laws can nullify a will. In some cases, holographic (handwritten) wills have actually been voided by notarization because the document was not entirely in the handwriting of the testator.

Avoid the Unauthorized Practice of Law. In a memorandum to Washington Notaries, dated September 19, 1985, the Attorney General advised that "a Notary may notarize the signatures upon, and statements of witnesses to, wills in which the Notary has no beneficial interest and when the Notary is not one of the persons whose signature or statement is being notarized.

"However, a Notary should not render advice upon legal questions, such as the validity of a will, the required form for a witness' statement, the number of witnesses required to make a will valid in this state or the effectiveness of any of the provisions of the will. These types of questions should be referred to an attorney. If a Notary attempts to answer them, and the Notary is wrong resulting in loss or damage to any person, the Notary may be held to the standard of an attorney in any subsequent legal action. Further, depending upon the circumstances, the Notary may be found to have engaged in the unauthorized practice of law."

Do Not Proceed Without Certificate Wording. A Notary should notarize a will only if a notarial certificate is provided for each signer, and the signers are not asking questions about how to proceed. Any such questions should be answered by an attorney.

Living Wills. Documents that are popularly called living wills may be notarized. These are not actually wills at all, but written statements of the signer's wishes concerning medical treatment in the event that the signer has an illness or injury and is unable to issue instructions on his or her own behalf.

MISCONDUCT, FINES AND PENALTIES

Misconduct

Misconduct Defined. Official misconduct generally takes place when a Washington Notary performs an act that is prohibited by law, or fails to perform an act that is required by law. The Notary's appointment is subject to revocation, suspension or denial by the Department of Licensing (RCW 42.44.030 and 42.44.160).

Serious Crime Defined. A serious crime is defined as any crime that involves false swearing, misrepresentation, fraud, unauthorized practice of law, deceit, bribery, extortion, misappropriation, theft, conspiracy, interference with the administration of justice or the solicitation of another to commit a crime (RCW 42.44.010).

Qualification and Maintenance of Appointment

Cause for Denial. The Department of Licensing may deny a notarial appointment for the following reasons (RCW 42.44.030):

- Conviction of a serious crime

- Revocation, suspension or restriction of a Notary appointment or other professional license in Washington or any other state

- Engaging in official misconduct, whether or not criminal penalties resulted

- Performance of a notarial act in a manner that would constitute negligence or disregard for the notarial office

Revocation. The Department of Licensing may revoke a Notary's appointment for any one of the following reasons (RCW 42.44.030 and 42.44.170):

- Conviction of a serious crime

- Suspension or revocation of a professional license in Washington or any other state

- Knowingly completing a false certificate

- Performing a notarial act in a negligent manner

- Having been deemed incompetent by judicial finding

Judgment of Incompetence by Judicial Finding. The Department of Licensing may revoke a Notary's appointment if the Notary is found incompetent by a court. In this case, the Notary's guardian or conservator must deliver a letter of resignation within 30 days of judgment to the Department of Licensing on behalf of the Notary. The letter must be accompanied by the Notary's seal or stamp (RCW 42.44.170).

Failure to Maintain Commission Qualifications. A Notary who fails to maintain the qualifications of a Notary appointment is subject to commission revocation (WAC 308-30-150). (See "How to Become a Washington Notary Public," pages 3-5.)

Action on Other Professional License. A Notary applicant who has had a professional license revoked, suspended, restricted or denied as a result of misconduct, dishonesty or similar causes is subject to having the Notary appointment revoked or denied (RCW 42.44.030).

Conviction of Felony or Crime of Moral Turpitude. A Notary who is convicted of a felony or crime involving moral turpitude may have his or her appointment revoked, suspended or denied by the Department of Licensing (RCW 42.44.030).

Must Report Conviction. Within 30 days of having been convicted of a felony or lesser offense — such as falsifying records, false swearing and giving false information, etc. — the Notary must file a written statement with the Department of Licensing. The statement must contain: the Notary's name, appointment number and appointment expiration date; the type of conviction and sentence; and the court and jurisdiction in which the Notary was convicted. Judgments against the Notary for any civil action should also be reported (WAC 308-30-140).

Illegal and Improper Acts

Impersonating a Notary. A person who does not have a valid Notary appointment or who impersonates a Notary is guilty of a gross misdemeanor (RCW 42.44.160).

Unauthorized Practice of Law. A Notary may not give legal advice or accept fees for legal advice. A nonattorney Notary is generally not permitted to assist other persons in drafting, preparing, completing or understanding a document or transaction. A Notary who engages in the unauthorized practice of law is guilty of a misdemeanor (RCW 2.48.170, 2.48.180 and WAC 308-30-090). (See "Unauthorized Practice of Law," page 55.)

Notarize Own Signature. Notaries are not permitted to notarize their own signatures (RCW 42.44.080). The NNA recommends against notarizing documents in which they are named.

False Certificate. In completing a false certificate — for example, stating a signer appeared when he or she actually did not — a Notary may be guilty of a gross misdemeanor (RCW 42.20.050 and 42.44.160).

Completing False Document. A Notary who falsely completes a document may be guilty of forgery with intent to deceive or defraud, a Class C Felony (RCW 9A.60.020).

Failure to Require Personal Appearance. A Notary may not notarize any document without the signer personally appearing before the Notary. Since notarial certificate wording specifies that the signer appeared before the Notary at the time of notarization, failing to require such personal appearance is considered completion of a false certificate, a gross misdemeanor (RCW 42.20.050 and 42.44.160).

Endorsements and Testimonials. Notaries may not use their seals or the title Notary Public except in performing notarial acts. A Notary may not promote or endorse any product, service, contest, candidate or other offering (WAC 308-30-160).

Overcharging. A Notary may not charge more than the maximum fees allowed by law. Charging more than the prescribed maximum fees is considered requesting unlawful compensation, a Class C Felony (RCW 9A.68.020).

Fees Not Posted. Notaries must post the notarization fee schedule in a conspicuous area in their place of business, or present it to each customer outside their business, in no smaller than 10-point type (WAC 308-30-020).

Copies of Naturalization Certificates Prohibited. The law imposes harsh penalties for printing or photographing a certificate of naturalization without lawful authority. The NNA recommends that a Notary only certify a copy of a certificate of naturalization if written directions are provided by a U.S. immigration authority.

Signature under Duress. No person, including a Notary, may force a person to sign a document. A person is guilty of obtaining a signature by deception or duress, a Class C Felony, if by intending to deceive or defraud, he or she causes the signer to execute an instrument (RCW 9A.60.030).

Failure to Perform Duty. A public servant, such as a Notary, is guilty of official misconduct and a gross misdemeanor if failing to fully and faithfully perform duties prescribed by law (RCW 9A.80.010).

Duty Performed by Another for Profit. No public officer may willingly grant authority to, or accept a fee from, another person who intends to exercise the duties of that public office (RCW 42.20.020).

Notary Seal or Stamp
Disposition of the Notary's Seal/Stamp. Upon revocation,

suspension, restriction or resignation of the Notary's commission, the Notary seal or inking stamp must be delivered to the Department of Licensing (WAC 308-30-040).

When a Notary resigns the commission, the Notary seal or stamp must be filed with the Department of Licensing at the same time the Notary files the letter of resignation (WAC 308-30-040).

When a commission expires naturally after the four-year term, the Notary is not required to submit the seal or stamp to the Department of Licensing but should destroy the seal or stamp as soon as possible to eliminate the chance of fraudulent misuse.

Should the Notary die during the commission term, the Notary's personal representative should destroy the seal or stamp. Any notarial records (e.g., the journal) should be retained at least until the statute of limitations expires.

Unauthorized Manufacturing of Seal. It is unlawful to manufacture, give, sell, buy or possess a Notary seal or stamp if the Department of Licensing has not issued a Certificate of Appointment. Further, a Notary may not obtain a seal or stamp from a manufacturer without first presenting a photocopy of the Certificate of Appointment or duplicate Certificate in the case of a name change (RCW 42.44.050 and WAC 308-30-010).

Seal Exclusive Property of Notary. A Notary's seal or stamp is the exclusive property of the Notary named on it. The seal or stamp may not be used by any other person or surrendered to an employer upon termination of employment (RCW 42.44.090).

Investigation and Appeal

Liable for All Damages. A person who is injured by the Notary's misconduct or negligence may file a lawsuit against the Notary for the full extent of damages.

Notary errors and omissions insurance, however, provides protection for a Notary who is sued for damages resulting from unintentional mistakes made while performing notarial acts. Such insurance is optional and is available from many sources. Errors and omissions insurance does not cover the Notary for intentional misconduct.

Denial of Appointment. Should a Notary wish to appeal a denial or revocation of his or her appointment, he or she must

submit a notice in writing and mail or deliver it to the Department
of Licensing. The written notice of appeal must be received
by the Department within 20 days of the date of denial or
revocation, or the applicant will lose the right to appeal
(WAC 308-30-080). ■

Digital Signatures

Electronic Transactions

Electronic Authentication Act. The Washington Electronic Authentication Act (RCW Chapter 19.34), which took effect May 13, 1999, is a technology-specific electronic transactions and signature law that requires the use of public key certificates supported by a public key infrastructure (PKI). Public key certificates are issued to individual users and are used to sign electronic documents.

Electronic Notarization

Purpose. While a paper document is signed by pen and ink, an electronic document — any message stored on a computer, such as a letter or other type of personal paper — may be signed by an elaborately encoded message called a digital signature.

Digital signatures are based on a technology known as Public Key Infrastructure (PKI), whereby two persons may communicate and conduct business between two computer terminals using coded messages. These coded messages are unreadable and unchangeable without special public and private keys assigned to the users. This exchange of electronic documents between computer terminals is called Electronic Data Interchange or EDI.

Public Keys and Private Keys. Electronic messages sent between computers may be digitally signed and authenticated through public key cryptography, which involves key pairs, each consisting of a unique public key and private key.

To send an electronic message, the author/signer scrambles the text with the intended recipient's public key. Once coded, this message can only be decoded with the recipient's private key. This allows the recipient to know if the original message was changed or tampered with in any way.

Public and private keys are registered through state-authorized certification authorities.

Digital Signatures

Raising awareness. Notaries should be aware of the increasingly popular use of digital signatures in domestic and international commerce. Washington is one of sixteen states leading the way, recognizing the legal validity of digital signatures and establishing procedures for regulation of certification authorities.

Uniform Real Property Electronic Recording Act (URPERA). Washington has adopted the Uniform Real Property Electronic Recording Act (RCW Title 65, as yet uncodified), which permits a Notary to use an electronic signature to notarize an electronic document without affixing an image of the Notary's official physical seal. This act is reprinted in its entirety in "Laws Pertaining to Washington Notaries," pages 100-102.

Test Your Knowledge

Trial Exam

Instructions. This examination is designed to test your knowledge of the basic concepts of notarization. Work through the exam without looking at the answers, then check your responses and note where you need additional study. Careful review of "Notary Laws Explained" (pages 18–68), the reprinted Notary statutes (RCW) and Administrative Code regulations (WAC) (pages 77-107), "10 Most-Asked Questions" (pages 8–12) and "Steps to Proper Notarization" (pages 13–17) will produce the answers.

A perfect score on this examination is 100 points. There are:

- 20 true/false questions worth one point each.
- 5 multiple-choice questions worth four points each.
- 5 fill-in-the-blank questions worth four points each.
- 5 essay questions worth eight points each.

Now, get a separate sheet of paper and a pen or pencil, and prepare to test your knowledge.

Part 1: True/False. For the following statements, answer true or false. Each correct answer is worth one point:

1. Notaries may act only in the county where they are commissioned. True or false?

2. The maximum Notary fee for taking the acknowledgment of three signers is $15. True or false?

3. It is a Notary's duty to serve all persons requesting lawful notarial acts, unless the Notary's employer has a policy stating otherwise. True or false?

4. Notaries must keep a photocopy of every document notarized. True or false?

5. A deposition is oral testimony that is written down and used as evidence in a court proceeding. True or false?

6. Notaries can withhold their services if they believe a signer is incoherent and unable to understand a document. True or false?

7. Upon request, it is a Notary's duty to draft powers of attorney, mortgages and deeds. True or false?

8. The letters "L.S." stand for the Latin words *locus sigilli*, which mean "location of the seal." True or false?

9. Holographic wills must be notarized to be valid. True or false?

10. A credible witness vouches for the identity of a signer in the Notary's presence. True or false?

11. Notaries may notarize documents executed by the company that employs them. True or false?

12. A Notary who does not charge fees is not required to post a fee schedule. True or false?

13. The Notary need not reimburse the insurance company for E&O insurance funds paid out to a person financially harmed by the Notary's actions. True or false?

14. A Notary is not required to verify that a sworn signer has the authority to sign as a corporate officer. True or false?

15. A Notary's seal and journal belong to the Notary's employer if the employer paid for them. True or false?

16. An acknowledgment certificate is not to be used for jurats. True or false?

17. An affirmation is the legal equivalent of an oath but makes no reference to a Supreme Being. True or false?

18. If presented with a document that does not include notarial wording, the Notary should automatically attach and complete an acknowledgment. True or false?

19. Notaries may not refuse to notarize blank or incomplete documents if they are signed in the Notary's presence. True or false?

20. A Notary may notarize a deed in which the Notary is named. True or false?

<u>Multiple Choice</u>. Choose the one best answer to each question. Each correct answer is worth 4 points.

1. A Notary has a disqualifying interest when acting as...
   a. A legal secretary typing papers under the instruction of an employer-attorney for a client.
   b. A bank employee preparing loan documents.
   c. A real estate agent selling a condominium and getting a commission.

2. To become a Notary, an applicant must ...
   a. Have been a state resident for at least one year.
   b. Be at least 18 years old.
   c. Pass an oral exam given by the Governor's office.

3. A certificate of authority for a Notary may be obtained...
   a. From the Governor's office or the county clerk.
   b. From a stationery store or the Notary himself/herself.
   c. From the Department of Licensing.

4. "Satisfactory evidence" of identity means reliance on...
   a. ID cards only.
   b. Personal knowledge of identity only.
   c. A credible witness or ID cards.

5. A Washington Notary may ...
   _e_ a. Take verifications under oath or affirmation.
      b. Correct errors in the document being notarized.
      c. Certify a copy of a foreign birth certificate.

<u>Fill in the Blank</u>. Write in the word or phrase that best completes each sentence. Each correct answer is worth four points.

1. A Notary bond protects the public while _E+O_ insurance protects the Notary.

2. A solemn, spoken pledge that is not an affirmation is called an _Oath_.

3. An acceptable ID card should contain a signature, physical description and _photo_ of its bearer.

4. A certified copy certifies the _accuracy_ of the reproduction.

5. Wills written entirely in the testator's own handwriting are called _Holographic_

<u>Essay</u>. Reply to each question or statement with a short paragraph. Each complete and correct response is worth eight points.

1. Discuss the reasons to obtain Notary errors and omissions insurance.

2. How does a proof of acknowledgment by subscribing witness work?

3. What is an _apostille_ and when is it used?

4. Why should a Notary always complete the journal entry before filling out a notarial certificate?

5. Outline the differences between an acknowledgment certificate and a jurat.

Test Answers

<u>True/False</u>. 1. F; 2. F; 3. F; 4. F; 5. T; 6. T; 7. F; 8. T; 9. F; 10. T; 11. T; 12. T; 13. T; 14. T; 15. F; 16. T; 17. T; 18. F; 19. F; 20. F

<u>Multiple Choice</u>. 1. c; 2. b; 3. c; 4. c; 5. a

<u>Fill in the Blank</u>. 1. Errors and omissions; 2. Oath; 3. Photograph; 4. Accuracy; 5. Holographic.

<u>Essay</u>. Responses should include the basic information in the paragraphs below:

1. Notary errors and omissions insurance protects Notaries from actions against them for unintentional errors. Purchased from a state-licensed company, Notary errors and omissions insurance protects the Notary in case of such an unintentional error, but only up to the policy limit. The Notary is not required to reimburse the insurance company.

2. A proof of acknowledgment by subscribing witness is sometimes used when a real estate document's principal signer is unavailable to appear before a Notary. In most such cases, the principal will be out of town, out of state, or even out of the country. A subscribing witness who has either seen the principal sign the document or has taken the principal's acknowledgment of the signature may present this document to a Notary on the principal's behalf. The witness must sign (subscribe) the document in addition to the principal. The witness, who must be personally known to the Notary, is given an oath by the Notary. A person who is a grantee or beneficiary of a document should not serve as a subscribing witness. While proofs of execution by subscribing witness are not prohibited by Washington law, their use is generally discouraged by state officials because of the increased potential for fraud.

3. An *apostille* is a certificate authenticating the signature and seal/stamp of a Notary. It is issued under provisions of an international treaty, signed by more than 90 nations, called the *Hague Convention Abolishing the Requirement of Legalization for Foreign Public Documents.* For notarized

documents exchanged between the subscribing nations, this treaty streamlines the time-consuming authentication process known as chain certification by requiring only one authenticating certificate, the *apostille* (French for "notation"). *Apostilles* for Washington Notaries are issued by the Department of Licensing's Notary Section.

4. Filling out a journal entry before completing a notarial certificate prevents a signer from leaving with the document before an important record of the notarization is made in the journal.

5. An acknowledgment certificate certifies that the signer of the document personally appeared before the Notary on the date and in the county indicated. It also certifies that the signer's identity was satisfactorily proven to the Notary, and that the signer acknowledged having signed freely. A jurat certifies that the person signing the document did so in the Notary's presence, that the person appeared before the Notary on the date and in the county indicated and that the Notary administered an oath or affirmation to the signer. For a jurat, the Notary also must positively identify the signer.

Tally Your Score

After checking your answers, add up your score. Then look at the grading scale below to determine how you stand:

- 90–100: Excellent!
- 80–89: Good, but some review needed.
- 70–79: Fair. Reread the parts of the *Primer* covering the answers you missed.
- Below 70: Subpar. Study the laws thoroughly again. ■

Washington Laws Pertaining to Notaries Public

Reprinted on the following pages is the complete text of the enacted laws and administrative regulations affecting Notaries and notarial acts, drawn from the Revised Code of Washington (RCW) and the Washington Administrative Code (WAC). Citations in brackets at the end of each section indicate the legislative history of the section.

Revised Code of Washington
CHAPTER 42.44 RCW
NOTARIES PUBLIC

Sections

42.44.010	Definitions.
42.44.020	Qualifications—Application—Bond.
42.44.030	Appointment — Denial for unprofessional conduct — Certificate of appointment.
42.44.040	Repealed.
42.44.050	Seal or stamp.
42.44.060	Term.
42.44.070	Reappointment without endorsements.
42.44.080	Standards for notarial acts.
42.44.090	Form of certificate—General—Seal or stamp as exclusive property.
42.44.100	Short forms of certificate.
42.44.110	Illegible writing.
42.44.120	Fees.
42.44.130	Notarial acts by officials of other jurisdictions.
42.44.140	Notarial acts by federal authorities.
42.44.150	Notarial acts by foreign authorities.
42.44.160	Official misconduct—Penalty.
42.44.170	Revocation of appointment—Resignation.
42.44.180	Evidence of authenticity of notarial seal and signature.
42.44.190	Rules.

42.44.200   Transfer of records.
42.44.900   Savings—1985 c 156.
42.44.901   Construction.
42.44.902   Severability—1985 c 156.
42.44.903   Effective date—1985 c 156.

RCW 42.44.010 Definitions. Unless the context clearly requires otherwise, the definitions in this section apply throughout this chapter.

(1) "Director" means the director of licensing of the state of Washington or the director's designee.

(2) "Notarial act" and "notarization" mean:

(a) Taking an acknowledgment;

(b) administering an oath or affirmation;

(c) taking a verification upon oath or affirmation;

(d) witnessing or attesting a signature;

(e) certifying or attesting a copy;

(f) receiving a protest of a negotiable instrument;

(g) certifying that an event has occurred or an act has been performed; and

(h) any other act that a notary public of this state is authorized to perform.

(3) "Notary public" and "notary" mean any person appointed to perform notarial acts in this state.

(4) "Acknowledgment" means a statement by a person that the person has executed an instrument as the person's free and voluntary act for the uses and purposes stated therein and, if the instrument is executed in a representative capacity, a statement that the person signed the document with proper authority and executed it as the act of the person or entity represented and identified therein.

(5) "Verification upon oath or affirmation" means a statement by a person who asserts it to be true and makes the assertion upon oath or affirmation administered in accordance with chapter 5.28 RCW.

(6) "In a representative capacity" means:

(a) For and on behalf of a corporation, partnership, trust, or other entity, as an authorized officer, agent, partner, trustee, or other representative;

(b) As a public officer, personal representative, guardian, or other representative, in the capacity recited in the instrument;

(c) As an attorney in fact for a principal; or

(d) In any other capacity as an authorized representative of another.

(7) "Serious crime" means any felony or any lesser crime, a necessary element of which, as determined by the statutory or common law definition of such crime, involves interference with the administration of justice, false swearing, misrepresentation, fraud, the unauthorized practice of law, deceit, bribery, extortion, misappropriation, theft, or an attempt, a conspiracy, or the solicitation of another to commit a serious crime. [1985 c 156 §1.]

RCW 42.44.020 Qualifications—Application—Bond. (1) The director may, upon application, appoint to be a notary public in this state, any person who:

(a) Is at least eighteen years of age;

(b) Resides in Washington state, or resides in an adjoining state and is regularly employed in Washington state or carries on business in Washington state; and

(c) Can read and write English.

(2) Each application shall be accompanied by endorsements by at least three residents of this state of the age of eighteen or more, who

are not relatives of the applicant, in the following form:

I, (name of endorser), being a person eligible to vote in the state of Washington, believe the applicant for a notary public appointment, (applicant's name), who is not related to me, to be a person of integrity and good moral character and capable of performing notarial acts.
_____ (Endorser's signature and address, with date of signing)

(3) Every application for appointment as a notary public shall be accompanied by a fee established by the director by rule.
(4) Every applicant for appointment as a notary public shall submit an application in a form prescribed by the director, and shall sign the following declaration in the presence of a notary public of this state:

Declaration of Applicant

I, (name of applicant), solemnly swear or affirm under penalty =of perjury that the personal information I have provided in this application is true, complete, and correct; that I carefully have read the materials provided with the application describing the duties of a notary public in and for the state of Washington; and, that I will perform, to the best of my ability, all notarial acts in accordance with the law.
_____ (Signature of applicant)

State of Washington
County of _____
On this day _____ appeared before me, signed this Declaration of Application, and swore (or affirmed) that (he/she) understood its contents and that its contents are truthful.
Dated: _____
_____ Signature of notary public   (Seal or stamp)
Residing at _____

(5) Every applicant shall submit to the director proof from a surety company that a ten thousand dollar surety bond, insuring the proper performance of notarial acts by the applicant, will be effective for a term commencing on the date the person is appointed, and expiring on the date the applicant's notary appointment expires. The surety for the bond shall be a company qualified to write surety bonds in this state. [1985 c 156 §2.]

RCW 42.44.030 Appointment — Denial for unprofessional conduct — Certificate of appointment. In addition to the unprofessional conduct specified in RCW 18.235.130, the director may deny appointment as a notary public to any person based on the following conduct, acts, or conditions:
(1) Has had disciplinary action taken against any professional license in this or any other state; or
(2) Has engaged in official misconduct as defined in RCW 42.44.160(1), whether or not criminal penalties resulted.
The director shall deliver a certificate evidencing the appointment to each person appointed as a notary public. The certificate may be signed in facsimile by the governor, the secretary of state, and the director or the director's designee. The certificate shall bear a printed seal of the state of Washington. [2002 c 86 § 287; 1985 c 156 § 3.]

RCW 42.44.040. Repealed.

RCW 42.44.050 Seal or stamp. Every person appointed as a notary public in this state shall procure a seal or stamp, on which shall be engraved or impressed the words "Notary Public" and "State of Washington," the date the appointment expires, the person's surname, and at least the initials of the person's first and middle names. The director shall prescribe by rule the size and form or forms of the seal or stamp. It is unlawful for any person intentionally to manufacture, give, sell, procure or possess a seal or stamp evidencing the current appointment of a person as a notary public until the director has delivered a certificate evidencing the appointment as provided for in RCW 42.44.040. [1985 c 156 §5.]

RCW 42.44.060 Term. A person appointed as a notary public by the director may perform notarial acts in this state for a term of four years, unless:
(1) The notarial appointment has been revoked under RCW 42.44.130 or 42.44.140; or
(2) The notarial appointment has been resigned. [1985 c 156 §6.]

RCW 42.44.070 Reappointment without endorsements. A person who has received an appointment as a notary public may be reappointed without the endorsements required in RCW 42.44.020(2) if the person submits a new application before the expiration date of the current appointment. [1985 c 156 §7.]

RCW 42.44.080 Standards for notarial acts. A notary public is authorized to perform notarial acts in this state. Notarial acts shall be performed in accordance with the following, as applicable:
(1) In taking an acknowledgment, a notary public must determine and certify, either from personal knowledge or from satisfactory evidence, that the person appearing before the notary public and making the acknowledgement is the person whose true signature is on the document.
(2) In taking an acknowledgment authorized by RCW 64.08.100 from a person physically unable to sign his or her name or make a mark, a notary public shall, in addition to other requirements for taking an acknowledgment, determine and certify from personal knowledge or satisfactory evidence that the person appearing before the notary public is physically unable to sign his or her name or make a mark and is otherwise competent. The notary public shall include in the acknowledgment a statement that the signature in the acknowledgment was obtained under the authority of RCW 64.08.100.
(3) In taking a verification upon oath or affirmation, a notary public must determine, either from personal knowledge or from satisfactory evidence, that the person appearing before the notary public and making the verification is the person whose true signature is on the statement verified.
(4) In witnessing or attesting a signature, a notary public must determine, either from personal knowledge or from satisfactory evidence, that the signature is that of the person appearing before the notary public and named in the document.
(5) In certifying or attesting a copy of a document or other item, a notary public must determine that the proffered copy is a full, true, and accurate transcription or reproduction of that which was copied.
(6) In making or noting a protest of a negotiable instrument, a notary public must determine the matters set forth in *RCW 62A.3-509.
(7) In certifying that an event has occurred or an act has been performed, a notary public must determine the occurrence or performance either from personal knowledge or from satisfactory evidence based upon the oath or affirmation of a credible witness personally known to the notary public.

(8) A notary public has satisfactory evidence that a person is the person described in a document if that person: (a) Is personally known to the notary public; (b) is identified upon the oath or affirmation of a credible witness personally known to the notary public; or (c) is identified on the basis of identification documents.

(9) The signature and seal or stamp of a notary public are prima facie evidence that the signature of the notary is genuine and that the person is a notary public.

(10) A notary public is disqualified from performing a notarial act when the notary is a signer of the document which is to be notarized. [1987 c 76 §3; 1985 c 156 §8.]

Reviser's note: RCW 62A.3-509 was repealed by 1993 c 229 §76, effective July 1, 1994.

RCW 42.44.090 Form of certificate—General—Seal or stamp as exclusive property. (1) A notarial act by a notary public must be evidenced by a certificate signed and dated by a notary public. The certificate must include the name of the jurisdiction in which the notarial act is performed and the title of the notary public or other notarial officer and shall be accompanied by an impression of the official seal or stamp. It shall not be necessary for a notary public in certifying an oath to be used in any of the courts in this state, to append an impression of the official seal or stamp. If the notarial officer is a notary public, the certificate shall also indicate the date of expiration of such notary public's appointment, but omission of that information may subsequently be corrected.

(2) A certificate of a notarial act is sufficient if it meets the requirements of subsection (1) of this section and it:

(a) Is in the short form set forth in RCW 42.44.100;

(b) Is in a form otherwise permitted or prescribed by the laws of this state;

(c) Is in a form prescribed by the laws or regulations applicable in the place in which the notarial act was performed; or

(d) Is in a form that sets forth the actions of the notary public and the described actions are sufficient to meet the requirements of the designated notarial act.

If any law of this state specifically requires a certificate in a form other than that set forth in RCW 42.44.100 in connection with a form of document or transaction, the certificate required by such law shall be used for such document or transaction.

(3) By executing a certificate of a notarial act, the notary public certifies that he or she has made the determinations required by RCW 42.44.080.

(4) A notary public's seal or stamp shall be the exclusive property of the notary public, shall not be used by any other person, and shall not be surrendered to an employer upon termination of employment, regardless of whether the employer paid for the seal or for the notary's bond or appointment fees. [1985c 156 §9.]

RCW 42.44.100 Short forms of certificate. The following short forms of notarial certificates are sufficient for the purposes indicated, if completed with the information required by this section:

(1) For an acknowledgment in an individual capacity:

State of Washington
County of _____
     I certify that I know or have satisfactory evidence that (name of person) is the person who appeared before me, and said person acknowledged that (he/she) signed this instrument and acknowledged it to be (his/her) free and voluntary act for the uses and purposes mentioned in the instrument.
Dated: _____
(Signature)   (Seal or stamp)
Title _____
My appointment expires _____

(2) For an acknowledgment in a representative capacity:

State of Washington
County of _____
     I certify that I know or have satisfactory evidence that (name of person) is the person who appeared before me, and said person acknowledged that (he/she) signed this instrument, on oath stated that (he/she) was authorized to execute the instrument and acknowledged it as the (type of authority, e.g., officer, trustee, etc.) of (name of party on behalf of whom instrument was executed) to be the free and voluntary act of such party for the uses and purposes mentioned in the instrument.
Dated: _____
(Signature)   (Seal or stamp)
Title _____
My appointment expires _____

(3) For a verification upon oath or affirmation:

State of Washington
County of _____
     Signed and sworn to (or affirmed) before me on (date) by (name of person making statement).
(Signature)   (Seal or stamp)
Title _____
My appointment expires _____

(4) For witnessing or attesting a signature:

State of Washington
County of _____
     Signed or attested before me on _____ by _____.
(Signature)   (Seal or stamp)
Title _____
My appointment expires _____

(5) For attestation of a copy of a document:

State of Washington
County of _____
     I certify that this is a true and correct copy of a document in the possession of _____ as of this date.

Dated: _____
(Signature)   (Seal or stamp)
Title _____
My appointment expires _____

(6) For certifying the occurrence of an event or the performance of an act:

State of Washington
County of _____
        I certify that the event or act described in this document has
occurred or been performed.
Dated: _____
(Signature)   (Seal or stamp)
Title _____
My appointment expires _____

[1988 c 69 §4; 1985 c 156 §10.]

RCW 42.44.110 Illegible writing. The illegibility of any wording, writing, or marking required under this chapter does not in and of itself affect the validity of a document or transaction. [1985 c 156 §11.]

RCW 42.44.120 Fees. (1) The director shall establish by rule the maximum fees that may be charged by notaries public for various notarial services.
(2) A notary public need not charge fees for notarial acts. [1985 c 156 §12.]

RCW 42.44.130 Notarial acts by officials of other jurisdictions. (1) A notarial act has the same effect under the law of this state as if performed by a notary public of this state, if performed in another state, commonwealth, territory, district, or possession of the United States by any of the following persons:
(a) A notary public of that jurisdiction;
(b) A judge, clerk, or deputy clerk of a court of that jurisdiction; or
(c) Any other person authorized by the law of that jurisdiction to perform notarial acts.
Notarial acts performed in other jurisdictions of the United States under federal authority as provided in RCW 42.44.140 have the same effect as if performed by a notarial officer of this state.
(2) The signature and title of a person performing a notarial act are prima facie evidence that the signature is genuine and that the person holds the designated title.
(3) The signature and title of an officer listed in subsection (1) (a) and (b) of this section conclusively establish the authority of a holder of that title to perform a notarial act. [1985 c 156 §13.]

RCW 42.44.140 Notarial acts by federal authorities. (1) A notarial act has the same effect under the law of this state as if performed by a notary public of this state if performed by any of the following persons under authority granted by the law of the United States:
(a) A judge, clerk, or deputy clerk of a court;
(b) A commissioned officer in active service with the military forces of the United States;
(c) An officer of the foreign service or consular agent of the United States; or

(d) Any other person authorized by federal law to perform notarial acts.

(2) The signature and title of a person performing a notarial act are prima facie evidence that the signature is genuine and that the person holds the designated title.

(3) The signature and title or rank of an officer listed in subsection (1) (a), (b), and (c) of this section conclusively establish the authority of a holder of that title to perform a notarial act. [1985 c 156 §14.]

RCW 42.44.150 Notarial acts by foreign authorities. (1) A notarial act has the same effect under the law of this state as if performed by a notary public of this state if performed within the jurisdiction of and under authority of a foreign nation or its constituent units or a multinational or international organization by any of the following persons:

(a) A notary public or notary;

(b) A judge, clerk, or deputy clerk of a court of record; or

(c) Any other person authorized by the law of that jurisdiction to perform notarial acts.

(2) An "apostille" in the form prescribed by the Hague Convention of October 5, 1961, conclusively establishes that the signature of the notarial officer is genuine and that the officer holds the designated office.

(3) A certificate by a foreign service or consular officer of the United States stationed in the nation under the jurisdiction of which the notarial act was performed, or a certificate by a foreign service or consular officer of that nation stationed in the United States, is prima facie evidence of the authenticity or validity of the notarial act set forth in the certificate.

(4) A stamp or seal of the person performing the notarial act is prima facie evidence that the signature is genuine and that the person holds that designated title.

(5) A stamp or seal of an officer listed in subsection (1) (a) or (b) of this section is prima facie evidence that a person with that title has authority to perform notarial acts.

(6) If the title of officer and indication of authority to perform notarial acts appears either in a digest of foreign law or in a list customarily used as a source for that information, the authority of an officer with that title to perform notarial acts is conclusively established. [1985 c 156 §15.]

RCW 42.44.160 Official misconduct—Penalty. (1) A notary public commits official misconduct when he or she signs a certificate evidencing a notarial act, knowing that the contents of the certificate are false.

(2) A notary public who commits an act of official misconduct shall be guilty of a gross misdemeanor.

(3) Any person not appointed as a notary public who acts as or otherwise impersonates a notary public shall be guilty of a gross misdemeanor. [1985 c 156 §16.]

RCW 42.44.170 Revocation of appointment—Resignation. (1) The director may revoke the appointment of any notary public for any reason for which appointment may be denied under RCW 42.44.030.

(2) The director shall revoke the appointment of a notary public upon a judicial finding of incompetency of the notary public. If a notary public is found to be incompetent, his or her guardian or conservator shall within

thirty days of such finding mail or deliver to the director a letter of resignation on behalf of the notary public.

(3) A notary public may voluntarily resign by mailing or delivering to the director a letter of resignation. [1985 c 156 §17.]

RCW 42.44.180 Evidence of authenticity of notarial seal and signature.

(1) The authenticity of the notarial seal and official signature of a notary public of this state may be evidenced by:

(a) A certificate of authority from the director or the secretary of state; or

(b) An apostille in the form prescribed by the Hague Convention Abolishing the Requirement of Legalization for Foreign Public Documents of October 5, 1961.

(2) An apostille as specified by the Hague Convention shall be attached to any document requiring authentication that is sent to a nation that has signed and ratified the Hague Convention Abolishing the Requirement of Legalization for Foreign Public Documents. [1985 c 156 §18.]

RCW 42.44.190 Rules. On or before January 1, 1986, the director shall adopt rules to carry out this chapter. Such rules shall include but shall not be limited to rules concerning applications for appointment, application and renewal fees, fees chargeable for notarial services, the replacement of lost or stolen seals or stamps, changes of names or addresses of notaries, resignations of notaries, appeals of denials and revocations of appointments, and issuance of evidences of authenticity of notarial seals and signatures. [1985 c 156 §20.]

RCW 42.44.200 Transfer of records. Records relating to the appointment and commissioning of notaries public that are in the custody of county clerks of this state on *the effective date of this act shall be transferred to the director of licensing on or before December 31, 1985. Such records may be archived by the director. [1985 c 156 §22.]

__Reviser's note:__ As used in this section, the phrase "the effective date of this act," is ambiguous; see RCW 42.44.903.

RCW 42.44.900 Savings—1985 c 156. Nothing in *this act may be interpreted to revoke any notary public appointment or commission existing on January 1, 1986. *This act does not terminate, or in any way modify, any liability, civil or criminal, which exists on January 1, 1986. A notarial act performed before January 1, 1986, is not affected by *this act. [1985 c 156 §21.]

__Reviser's note:__ "This act" [1985 c 156] consisted of the enactment of RCW 42.44.010 through 42.44.200 and 42.44.900 through 42.44.903, the amendment of RCW 43.07.035, and the repeal of chapter 42.28 RCW and RCW 43.06.100, 43.131.299, and 43.131.300.

RCW 42.44.901 Construction. RCW 42.44.010, 42.44.080, 42.44.090, 42.44.100, 42.44.130, 42.44.140, and 42.44.150 shall be applied and construed to effectuate their general purpose to make the law uniform with respect to the subject of this chapter among states enacting such sections of this chapter. [1985 c 156 §23.]

RCW 42.44.902 Severability—1985 c 156. If any provision of this act or its application to any person or circumstance is held invalid, the remainder of the act or the application of the provision to other persons or circumstances is not affected. [1985c 156 §24.]

RCW 42.44.903 Effective date—1985 c 156. Sections 1 through 19, 21, and 23 through 26 shall take effect on January 1, 1986. [1985 c 156 §27.]

*Reviser's note: For translation of above references see Codification Tables, Volume 0.

Additional Pertinent Statutes

TITLE 2. COURTS OF RECORD
Chapter 2.48 State bar act.

RCW 2.48.170 Only active members may practice law. No person shall practice law in this state subsequent to the first meeting of the state bar unless he shall be an active member thereof as hereinbefore defined: PROVIDED, That a member of the bar in good standing in any other state or jurisdiction shall be entitled to appear in the courts of this state under such rules as the board of governors may prescribe. [1933 c 94 §13; RRS §138-13.]

NOTES: Rules of court: Admission—APR 5.

RCW 2.48.180 Definitions—Unlawful practice a crime—Cause for discipline—Unprofessional conduct—Defense—Injunction—Remedies—Costs—Attorneys' fees—Time limit for action.

(1) As used in this section:

(a) "Legal provider" means an active member in good standing of the state bar, and any other person authorized by the Washington state supreme court to engage in full or limited practice of law;

(b) "Nonlawyer" means a person to whom the Washington supreme court has granted a limited authorization to practice law but who practices law outside that authorization, and a person who is not an active member in good standing of the state bar, including persons who are disbarred or suspended from membership;

(c) "Ownership interest" means the right to control the affairs of a business, or the right to share in the profits of a business, and includes a loan to the business when the interest on the loan is based upon the income of the business or the loan carries more than a commercially reasonable rate of interest.

(2) The following constitutes unlawful practice of law:

(a) A nonlawyer practices law, or holds himself or herself out as entitled to practice law;

(b) A legal provider holds an investment or ownership interest in a business primarily engaged in the practice of law, knowing that a nonlawyer holds an investment or ownership interest in the business;

(c) A nonlawyer knowingly holds an investment or ownership interest in a business primarily engaged in the practice of law;

(d) A legal provider works for a business that is primarily engaged in the practice of law, knowing that a nonlawyer holds an investment or ownership interest in the business; or

(e) A nonlawyer shares legal fees with a legal provider.

(3) Unlawful practice of law is a crime. A single violation of this section is a gross misdemeanor. Each subsequent violation, whether alleged in the same or in subsequent prosecutions, is a class C felony.

(4) Nothing contained in this section affects the power of the courts to grant injunctive or other equitable relief or to punish as for contempt.

(5) Whenever a legal provider or a person licensed by the state in a business

or profession is convicted, enjoined, or found liable for damages or a civil penalty or other equitable relief under this section, the plaintiff's attorney shall provide written notification of the judgment to the appropriate regulatory or disciplinary body or agency.

(6) A violation of this section is cause for discipline and constitutes unprofessional conduct that could result in any regulatory penalty provided by law, including refusal, revocation,or suspension of a business or professional license, or right or admission to practice. Conduct that constitutes a violation of this section is unprofessional conduct in violation of RCW 18.130.180.

(7) In a proceeding under this section it is a defense if proven by the defendant by a preponderance of the evidence that, at the time of the offense, the conduct alleged was authorized by the rules of professional conduct or the admission to practice rules, or Washington business and professions licensing statutes or rules.

(8) Independent of authority granted to the attorney general, the prosecuting attorney may petition the superior court for an injunction against a person who has violated this chapter. Remedies in an injunctive action brought by a prosecuting attorney are limited to an order enjoining, restraining, or preventing the doing of any act or practice that constitutes a violation of this chapter and imposing a civil penalty of up to five thousand dollars for each violation. The prevailing party in the action may, in the discretion of the court, recover its reasonable investigative costs and the costs of the action including a reasonable attorney's fee. The degree of proof required in an action brought under this subsection is a preponderance of the evidence. An action under this subsection must be brought within three years after the violation of this chapter occurred. [1995 c 285 §26; 1989 c 117 §13; 1933 c 94 §14; RRS §138-14.]

NOTES: Rules of court: RLD 1.1(h). Effective date—1995 c 285: See RCW 48.30A.900. Severability—Effective date—1989 c 117: See RCW 19.154.901 and 19.154.902. Practicing law with disbarred attorney: RCW 2.48.220(9).

TITLE 5. EVIDENCE
Chapter 5.28 Oaths and affirmations.

RCW 5.28.010 Who may administer. Every court, judge, clerk of a court, or notary public, is authorized to take testimony in any action, suit or proceeding, and such other persons in particular cases as authorized by law. Every such court or officer is authorized to collect fees established under RCW 36.18.020 and 36.18.012 through 36.18.018 and to administer oaths and affirmations generally and to every such other person in such particular case as authorized. [1995 c 292 §1; 1987 c 202 §124; 2 H. C. §1693; 1869 p 378 §1; RRS §1264.]

RCW 5.28.020 How administered. An oath may be administered as follows: The person who swears holds up his hand, while the person administering the oath thus addresses him: "You do solemnly swear that the evidence you shall give in the issue (or matter) now pending between _____ and _____ shall be the truth, the whole truth, and nothing but the truth, so help you God." If the oath be administered to any other than a witness giving testimony, the form may be changed to: "You do solemnly swear you will true answers make to such questions as you may be asked," etc. [2 H. C. §1694; 1869 p 378 §2; RRS §1265.]

RCW 5.28.030 Form may be varied. Whenever the court or officer before which a person is offered as a witness is satisfied that he has a peculiar mode of swearing connected with or in addition to the usual form of administration, which, in witness' opinion, is more solemn or obligatory, the court or officer may, in its discretion, adopt that mode. [2 H. C. §1695; 1869 p 379 §3; RRS §1266.]

RCW 5.28.040 Form may be adapted to religious belief. When a person is sworn who believes in any other than the Christian religion, he may be sworn according to the peculiar ceremonies of his religion, if there be any such. [2 H. C. §1696; 1869 p 379 §4; RRS §1267.]

RCW 5.28.050 Form of affirmation. Any person who has conscientious scruples against taking an oath, may make his solemn affirmation, by assenting, when addressed, in the following manner: "You do solemnly affirm that," etc., as in RCW 5.28.020. [2 H. C.§1697; 1869 p 379 §5; RRS §1268.]

RCW 5.28.060 Affirmation equivalent to oath. Whenever an oath is required, an affirmation, as prescribed in RCW 5.28.050 is to be deemed equivalent thereto, and a false affirmation is to be deemed perjury, equally with a false oath. [2 H. C. §1698; 1869p 379 §6; RRS §1269.]

Chapter 5.52 Telegraphic communications.

RCW 5.52.050 Telegraphic copies as evidence. Except as hereinbefore otherwise provided, any instrument in writing, duly certified, under his hand and official seal, by a notary public, commissioner of deeds, or clerk of a court of record, to be genuine, within the personal knowledge of such officer, may, together with such certificate, be sent by telegraph and the telegraphic copy thereof shall, prima facie, only have the same force, effect and validity, in all respects whatsoever as the original, and the burden of proof shall rest with the party denying the genuineness, or due execution of the original. [Code 1881 §2356; 1865 p 75 §15; RRS §11349.]

TITLE 9A. WASHINGTON CRIMINAL CODE
Chapter 9A.60 Fraud.

RCW 9A.60.010 Definitions. The following definitions and the definitions of RCW 9A.56.010 are applicable in this chapter unless the context otherwise requires:
  (1) "Written instrument" means: (a) Any paper, document, or other instrument containing written or printed matter or its equivalent; or (b) any access device, as defined in RCW 9A.56.010(3), token, stamp, seal, badge, trademark, or other evidence or symbol of value, right, privilege, or identification;
  (2) "Complete written instrument" means one which is fully drawn with respect to every essential feature thereof;
  (3) "Incomplete written instrument" means one which contains some matter by way of content or authentication but which requires additional matter in order to render it a complete written instrument;
  (4) To "falsely make" a written instrument means to make or draw a complete or incomplete written instrument which purports to be authentic, but which is not authentic either because the ostensible maker is fictitious or because, if real, he did not authorize the making or drawing thereof;
  (5) To "falsely complete" a written instrument means to transform an incomplete written instrument into a complete one by adding or inserting

matter, without the authority of anyone entitled to grant it;

(6) To "falsely alter" a written instrument means to change, without authorization by anyone entitled to grant it, a written instrument, whether complete or incomplete, by means of erasure, obliteration, deletion, insertion of new matter, transposition of matter, or in any other manner;

(7) "Forged instrument" means a written instrument which has been falsely made, completed or altered. [1987 c 140 §5; 1975-'762nd ex.s. c 38 §12; 1975 1st ex.s. c 260 §9A.60.010.]

RCW 9A.60.020 Forgery. (1) A person is guilty of forgery if, with intent to injure or defraud:

(a) He falsely makes, completes, or alters a written instrument or;

(b) He possesses, utters, offers, disposes of, or puts off as true a written instrument which he knows to be forged.

(2) Forgery is a class C felony. [1975-'76 2nd ex.s. c 38 §13; 1975 1st ex.s. c 260 §9A.60.020.]

RCW 9A.60.030 Obtaining a signature by deception or duress. (1) A person is guilty of obtaining a signature by deception or duress if by deception or duress and with intent to defraud or deprive he causes another person to sign or execute a written instrument.

(2) Obtaining a signature by deception or duress is a class C felony. [1975-'76 2nd ex.s. c 38 §14; 1975 1st ex.s. c 260 §9A.60.030.]

RCW 9A.60.040 Criminal impersonation. (1) A person is guilty of criminal impersonation in the first degree if the person:

(a) Assumes a false identity and does an act in his or her assumed character with intent to defraud another or for any other unlawful purpose; or

(b) Pretends to be a representative of some person or organization or a public servant and does an act in his or her pretended capacity with intent to defraud another or for any other unlawful purpose.

(2) Criminal impersonation in the first degree is a gross misdemeanor.

(3) A person is guilty of criminal impersonation in the second degree if the person:

(a) Claims to be a law enforcement officer or creates an impression that he or she is a law enforcement officer; and

(b) Under circumstances not amounting to criminal impersonation in the first degree, does an act with intent to convey the impression that he or she is acting in an official capacity and a reasonable person would believe the person is a law enforcement officer.

(4) Criminal impersonation in the second degree is a misdemeanor. [1993 c 457 §1; 1975 1st ex.s. c 260 §9A.60.040.]

RCW 9A.60.050 False certification. (1) A person is guilty of false certification, if, being an officer authorized to take a proof or acknowledgment of an instrument which by law may be recorded, he knowingly certifies falsely that the execution of such instrument was acknowledged by any party thereto or that the execution thereof was proved.

(2) False certification is a gross misdemeanor. [1975-'76 2nd ex.s. c 38 §15; 1975 1st ex.s. c 260 §9A.60.050.]

Chapter 9A.68 Bribery and corrupt influence.

RCW 9A.68.020 Requesting unlawful compensation. (1) A public servant is guilty of requesting unlawful compensation if he requests a pecuniary benefit for the performance of an official action knowing that he is required to perform that action without compensation or at a level of compensation lower than that requested.

    (2) Requesting unlawful compensation is a class C felony. [1975 1st ex.s. c 260 §9A.68.020.]

Chapter 9A.80 Abuse of office.

RCW 9A.80.010 Official misconduct. (1) A public servant is guilty of official misconduct if, with intent to obtain a benefit or to deprive another person of a lawful right or privilege:

    (a) He intentionally commits an unauthorized act under color of law; or

    (b) He intentionally refrains from performing a duty imposed upon him by law.

    (2) Official misconduct is a gross misdemeanor. [1975-'76 2nd ex.s. c 38 §17; 1975 1st ex.s. c 260 §9A.80.010.]

TITLE 26. DOMESTIC RELATIONS
Chapter 26.04 Marriage.

RCW 26.04.150 Application for license—May be secured by mail—Execution and acknowledgment. Any person may secure by mail from the county auditor of the county in the state of Washington where he intends to be married, an application, and execute and acknowledge said application before a notary public. [1963 c 230 §2; 1939 c 204 §3; RRS §8450-2.]

TITLE 36. COUNTIES
Chapter 36.18 Fees of county officers.

RCW 36.18.010 Auditor's fees. County auditors or recording officers shall collect the following fees for their official services:

For recording instruments, for the first page eight and one-half by fourteen inches or less, five dollars; for each additional page eight and one-half by fourteen inches or less, one dollar; the fee for recording multiple transactions contained in one instrument will be calculated individually for each transaction requiring separate indexing as required under RCW 65.04.050;

For preparing and certifying copies, for the first page eight and one-half by fourteen inches or less, three dollars; for each additional page eight and one-half by fourteen inches or less, one dollar;

For preparing noncertified copies, for each page eight and one-half by fourteen inches or less, one dollar;

For administering an oath or taking an affidavit, with or without seal, two dollars;

For issuing a marriage license, eight dollars, (this fee includes taking necessary affidavits, filing returns, indexing, and transmittal of a record of the marriage to the state registrar of vital statistics) plus an additional five-dollar fee for use and support of the prevention of child abuse and neglect activities to be transmitted monthly to the state treasurer and deposited in the state general fund plus an additional ten-dollar fee to be transmitted monthly to the state treasurer and deposited in the state general fund. The legislature intends to appropriate an amount at least equal to the revenue generated by this fee for the purposes of the displaced homemaker act, chapter 28B.04 RCW;

For searching records per hour, eight dollars;

For recording plats, fifty cents for each lot except cemetery plats for which the charge shall be twenty-five cents per lot; also one dollar for each acknowledgment, dedication, and description: PROVIDED, That there shall be a minimum fee of twenty-five dollars per plat;

For recording of miscellaneous records not listed above, for the first page eight and one-half by fourteen inches or less, five dollars; for each additional page eight and one-half by fourteen inches or less, one dollar;

For modernization and improvement of the recording and indexing system, a surcharge as provided in RCW 36.22.170. [1996 c 143 §1; 1995 c 246 §37; 1991 c 26 §2. Prior: 1989 c 304 §1; 1989 c 204 §6; 1987 c 230 §1; 1985 c 44 §2; 1984 c 261 §4; 19821 st ex.s. c 15 §7; 1982 c 4 §12; 1977 ex.s. c 56 §1; 1967 c 26 §8; 1963 c 4 §36. 18.010; prior: 1959 c 263 §6; 1953 c 214 §2; 1951 c 51 §4; 1907 c 56 §1, part, p 92; 1903 c 151 §1, part, p 295; 1893 c 130 §1, part, p 423; Code 1881 §2086, part, p 358; 1869 p 369 §3; 1865 p 94 §1; part; 1863 p 391 §1, part, p 394; 1861 p 34 §1, part, p 37; 1854 p 368 §1, part, p 371; RRS §§497, part, 4105.]

TITLE 42. PUBLIC OFFICERS AND AGENCIES
Chapter 42.20 Misconduct of public officers.

RCW 42.20.020 Powers may not be delegated for profit. Every public officer who, for any reward, consideration or gratuity paid or agreed to be paid, shall, directly or indirectly, grant to another the right or authority to discharge any function of his office, or permit another to perform any of his duties, shall be guilty of a gross misdemeanor. [1909 c 249 §83; RRS §2335.]

Reviser's note: Caption for 1909 c 249 §83 reads as follows: "Sec. 83. Grant of Official Powers."

RCW 42.20.030 Intrusion into and refusal to surrender public office. Every person who shall falsely personate or represent any public officer, or who shall wilfully intrude himself into a public office to which he has not been duly elected or appointed, or who shall wilfully exercise any of the functions or perform any of the duties of such officer, without having duly qualified therefor, as required by law, or who, having been an executive or administrative officer, shall wilfully exercise any of the functions of his office after his right to do so has ceased, or wrongfully refuse to surrender the official seal or any books or papers appertaining to such office, upon the demand of his lawful successor, shall be guilty of a gross misdemeanor. [1909 c 249 §84; RRS §2336.]

NOTES: Impersonating a public officer: RCW 9A.60.040. Quo warranto: Chapter 7.56 RCW.

RCW 42.20.040 False report. Every public officer who shall knowingly make any false or misleading statement in any official report or statement, under circumstances not otherwise prohibited by law, shall be guilty of a gross misdemeanor. [1909 c 249 §98; RRS §2350.]

RCW 42.20.050 Public officer making false certificate. Every public officer who, being authorized by law to make or give a certificate or other writing, shall knowingly make and deliver as true such a certificate or writing containing any statement which he knows to be false, in a case where the punishment thereof is not expressly prescribed by law, shall be guilty of a gross misdemeanor. [1909 c 249 §128; RRS §2380.]

RCW 42.20.100 Failure of duty by public officer a misdemeanor.

Whenever any duty is enjoined by law upon any public officer or other person holding any public trust or employment, their wilful neglect to perform such duty, except where otherwise specially provided for, shall be a misdemeanor. [1909 c 249 §16; RRS §2268. Prior: Code 1881 §889; 1854 p 90 §82.]

NOTES: Official misconduct by public servant: RCW 9A.80.010.

TITLE 62A. UNIFORM COMMERCIAL CODE
Article 3. Negotiable Instruments.
(Formerly: Commercial paper)
Part 5 Dishonor.

RCW 62A.3-501 Presentment. (a) "Presentment" means a demand made by or on behalf of a person entitled to enforce an instrument (i) to pay the instrument made to the drawee or a party obliged to pay the instrument or, in the case of a note or accepted draft payable at a bank, to the bank, or (ii) to accept a draft made to the drawee.

(b) The following rules are subject to Article 4, agreement of the parties, and clearinghouse rules and the like:

(1) Presentment may be made at the place of payment of the instrument and must be made at the place of payment if the instrument is payable at a bank in the United States; may be made by any commercially reasonable means, including an oral, written, or electronic communication; is effective when the demand for payment or acceptance is received by the person to whom presentment is made; and is effective if made to any one of two or more makers, acceptors, drawees, or other payors.

(2) Upon demand of the person to whom presentment is made, the person making presentment must (i) exhibit the instrument, (ii) give reasonable identification and, if presentment is made on behalf of another person, reasonable evidence of authority to do so, and (iii) sign a receipt on the instrument for any payment made or surrender the instrument if full payment is made.

(3) Without dishonoring the instrument, the party to whom presentment is made may (i) return the instrument for lack of a necessary indorsement, or (ii) refuse payment or acceptance for failure of the presentment to comply with the terms of the instrument, an agreement of the parties, or other applicable law or rule.

(4) The party to whom presentment is made may treat presentment as occurring on the next business day after the day of presentment if the party to whom presentment is made has established a cut-off hour not earlier than 2:00 p.m. for the receipt and processing of instruments presented for payment or acceptance and presentment is made after the cut-off hour. [1993c 229 §61; 1965 ex.s. c 157 §3-501. Cf. former RCW sections: RCW 62.01.070, 62.01.089, 62.01.118, 62.01.129, 62.01.143,62.01.144, 62.01.150, 62.01.151, 62.01.152, 62.01.157, 62.01.158, and 62.01.186; 1955 c 35 §§62.01.070, 62.01.089, 62.01.118, 62.01.129, 62.01.143, 62.01.144, 62.01.150, 62.01.151, 62.01.152, 62.01.157, 62.01.158, and 62.01.186; prior: 1899 c 149 §§70, 89, 118, 129, 143, 144, 150, 151, 152, 157, 158, and 186; RRS §§3461, 3479, 3508, 3519, 3533, 3534, 3540, 3541, 3542, 3547, 3548, and 3576.]

NOTES: Recovery of attorneys' fees—Effective date—1993 c 229: See RCW 62A.11-111 and 62A.11-112.

RCW 62A.3-502 Dishonor. (a) Dishonor of a note is governed by the following rules:

(1) If the note is payable on demand, the note is dishonored if presentment is duly made to the maker and the note is not paid on the day of presentment.

(2) If the note is not payable on demand and is payable at or through a bank or the terms of the note require presentment, the note is dishonored if presentment is duly made and the note is not paid on the day it becomes payable or the day of presentment, whichever is later.

(3) If the note is not payable on demand and subsection (a)(2) does not apply, the note is dishonored if it is not paid on the day it becomes payable.

(b) Dishonor of an unaccepted draft other than a documentary draft is governed by the following rules:

(1) If a check is duly presented for payment to the payor bank otherwise than for immediate payment over the counter, the check is dishonored if the payor bank makes timely return of the check or sends timely notice of dishonor or nonpayment under RCW 62A.4-301or 62A.4-302, or becomes accountable for the amount of the check under RCW 62A.4-302.

(2) If a draft is payable on demand and subsection (b)(1) does not apply, the draft is dishonored if presentment for payment is duly made to the drawee and the draft is not paid on the day of presentment.

(3) If a draft is payable on a date stated in the draft, the draft is dishonored if (i) presentment for payment is duly made to the drawee and payment is not made on the day the draft becomes payable or the day of presentment, whichever is later, or (ii) presentment for acceptance is duly made before the day the draft becomes payable and the draft is not accepted on the day of presentment.

(4) If a draft is payable on elapse of a period of time after sight or acceptance, the draft is dishonored if presentment for acceptance is duly made and the draft is not accepted on the day of presentment.

(c) Dishonor of an unaccepted documentary draft occurs according to the rules stated in subsection (b) (2), (3), and (4), except that payment or acceptance may be delayed without dishonor until no later than the close of the third business day of the drawee following the day on which payment or acceptance is required by subsection (b) (2), (3), and (4).

(d) Dishonor of an accepted draft is governed by the following rules:

(1) If the draft is payable on demand, the draft is dishonored if presentment for payment is duly made to the acceptor and the draft is not paid on the day of presentment; or

(2) If the draft is not payable on demand, the draft is dishonored if presentment for payment is duly made to the acceptor and payment is not made on the day it becomes payable or the day of presentment, whichever is later.

(e) In any case in which presentment is otherwise required for dishonor under this section and presentment is excused under RCW 62A.3-504, dishonor occurs without presentment if the instrument is not duly accepted or paid.

(f) If a draft is dishonored because timely acceptance of the draft was not made and the person entitled to demand acceptance consents to a late acceptance, from the time of acceptance the draft is treated as never having been dishonored. [1993 c 229 §62; 1965 ex.s. c 157 §3-502. Cf. former RCW sections: RCW 62.01.007, 62.01.070, 62.01.089, 62.01.144, 62.01.150, 62.01.152, and 62.01.186; 1955 c 35 §§62.01.007, 62.01.070, 62.01.089,62.01.144, 62.01.150, 62.01.152, and 62.01.186; prior: 1899 c 149 §§7, 70, 89, 144, 150, 152, and 186; RRS §§3398, 3461, 3479, 3534, 3540,

3542, and 3576.]

NOTES: Recovery of attorneys' fees—Effective date—1993 c 229: See RCW 62A.11-111 and 62A.11-112.

RCW 62A.3-503 Notice of dishonor. (a) The obligation of an indorser stated in RCW 62A.3-415(a) and the obligation of a drawer stated in RCW 62A.3-414(d) may not be enforced unless (i) the indorser or drawer is given notice of dishonor of the instrument complying with this section or (ii) notice of dishonor is excused under RCW 62A.3-504(b).

(b) Notice of dishonor may be given by any person; may be given by any commercially reasonable means, including an oral, written, or electronic communication; and is sufficient if it reasonably identifies the instrument and indicates that the instrument has been dishonored or has not been paid or accepted. Return of an instrument given to a bank for collection is sufficient notice of dishonor.

(c) Subject to RCW 62A.3-504(c), with respect to an instrument taken for collection by a collecting bank, notice of dishonor must be given (i) by the bank before midnight of the next banking day following the banking day on which the bank receives notice of dishonor of the instrument, or (ii) by any other person within 30days following the day on which the person receives notice of dishonor. With respect to any other instrument, notice of dishonor must be given within 30 days following the day on which dishonor occurs. [1993 c 229 §63; 1965 ex.s. c 157 §3-503. Cf. former RCW sections: (i) RCW 62.01.071, 62.01.072, 62.01.075, 62.01.086, 62.01.144, 62.01.145, 62.01.146, 62.01.186, and 62.01.193; 1955 c 35 §§62.01.071, 62.01.072, 62.01.075, 62.01.086, 62.01.144, 62.01.145, 62.01.146, 62.01.186, and 62.01.193; prior: 1899 c 149 §§71, 72, 75, 86, 144, 145, 146, 186, and 193; RRS §§3462, 3463, 3466, 3476, 3534, 3535, 3536, 3576, and 3583. (ii) RCW 62.01.085; 1955 c 35 §62.01.085; prior: 1915 c 173 §1; 1899 c 149 §85; RRS §3475 1/2.]

NOTES: Recovery of attorneys' fees—Effective date—1993 c 229: See RCW 62A.11-111 and 62A.11-112.

RCW 62A.3-504 Excused presentment and notice of dishonor. (a) Presentment for payment or acceptance of an instrument is excused if (i) the person entitled to present the instrument cannot with reasonable diligence make presentment, (ii) the maker or acceptor has repudiated an obligation to pay the instrument or is dead or in insolvency proceedings, (iii) by the terms of the instrument presentment is not necessary to enforce the obligation of indorsers or the drawer, (iv) the drawer or indorser whose obligation is being enforced has waived presentment or otherwise has no reason to expect or right to require that the instrument be paid or accepted, or (v) the drawer instructed the drawee not to pay or accept the draft or the drawee was not obligated to the drawer to pay the draft.

(b) Notice of dishonor is excused if (i) by the terms of the instrument notice of dishonor is not necessary to enforce the obligation of a party to pay the instrument, or (ii) the party whose obligation is being enforced waived notice of dishonor. A waiver of presentment is also a waiver of notice of dishonor.

(c) Delay in giving notice of dishonor is excused if the delay was caused by circumstances beyond the control of the person giving the notice and the person giving the notice exercised reasonable diligence after the cause of the delay ceased to operate. [1993 c229 §64; 1965 ex.s. c 157 §3-504. Cf. former RCW sections: RCW 62.01.072, 62.01.073, 62.01.077, 62.01.078, and

62.01.145; 1955 c35 §§62.01.072, 62.01.073, 62.01.077, 62.01.078, and 62.01.145; prior: 1899 c 149 §§72, 73, 77, 78, and 145; RRS §§3463, 3464, 3468, 3469, and 3535.]

NOTES: Recovery of attorneys' fees—Effective date—1993 c 229: See RCW 62A.11-111 and 62A.11-112.

RCW 62A.3-505 Evidence of dishonor. (a) The following are admissible as evidence and create a presumption of dishonor and of any notice of dishonor stated:

(1) A document regular in form as provided in subsection (b) that purports to be a protest;

(2) A purported stamp or writing of the drawee, payor bank, or presenting bank on or accompanying the instrument stating that acceptance or payment has been refused unless reasons for the refusal are stated and the reasons are not consistent with dishonor;

(3) A book or record of the drawee, payor bank, or collecting bank, kept in the usual course of business which shows dishonor, even if there is no evidence of who made the entry.

(b) A protest is a certificate of dishonor made by a United States consul or vice-consul, or a notary public or other person authorized to administer oaths by the law of the place where dishonor occurs. It may be made upon information satisfactory to that person. The protest must identify the instrument and certify either that presentment has been made or, if not made, the reason why it was not made, and that the instrument has been dishonored by nonacceptance or nonpayment. The protest may also certify that notice of dishonor has been given to some or all parties. [1993 c 229 §65; 1965 ex.s. c 157 §3-505. Cf. former RCW sections: (i) RCW 62.01.072(3); 1955 c 35 §62.01.072; prior: 1899 c 149 §72; RRS §3463. (ii) RCW 62.01.074; 1955 c 35 §62.01.074; prior: 1899 c 149 §74; RRS §3465. (iii) RCW 62.01.133; 1955 c 35 §62.01.133; prior: 1899 c 149 §133; RRS §3523.]

NOTES: Recovery of attorneys' fees—Effective date—1993 c 229: See RCW 62A.11-111 and 62A.11-112.

RCW 62A.3-512 Credit cards—As identification—In lieu of deposit. A person may not record the number of a credit card given as identification under *RCW 62A.3-501(a)(2) or given as proof of credit worthiness when payment for goods or services is made by check or draft. Nothing in this section prohibits the recording of the number of a credit card given in lieu of a deposit to secure payment in the event of a default, loss, damage, or other occurrence. [1993 c 229 §66; 1990 c 203 §2.]

Reviser's note: The reference to RCW 62A.3-501(a)(2) appears erroneous. Reference to RCW 62A.3-501(b)(2) was apparently intended. Recovery of attorneys' fees—Effective date—1993 c 229: See RCW 62A.11-111 and 62A.11-112.

RCW 62A.3-515 Checks dishonored by nonacceptance or nonpayment; liability for interest; rate; collection costs and attorneys' fees; satisfaction of claim. (a) If a check as defined in RCW 62A.3-104 is dishonored by nonacceptance or nonpayment, the payee or holder of the check is entitled to collect a reasonable handling fee for each instrument. If the check is not paid within fifteen days and after the holder of the check sends a notice of dishonor as provided by RCW 62A.3-520 to the drawer at the drawer's last known address, and if the instrument does not provide for the payment of interest or collection costs and attorneys' fees, the drawer of the instrument is liable for payment of interest at the rate of twelve percent per annum from the date of dishonor, and cost of collection not to exceed forty dollars or the face amount of the check, whichever is less. In addition, in the event of court action on the check, the court, after notice and the expiration of the fifteen days, shall award reasonable attorneys' fees, and three times the face amount of the check or three hundred dollars, whichever is less, as part of the damages payable to the holder of the check. This section does not apply to an instrument that is dishonored by reason of a justifiable stop payment order.

(b)(1) Subsequent to the commencement of an action on the check (subsection (a)) but prior to the hearing, the defendant may tender to the plaintiff as satisfaction of the claim, an amount of money equal to the face amount of the check, a reasonable handling fee, accrued interest, collection costs equal to the face amount of the check not to exceed forty dollars, and the incurred court costs, service costs, and statutory attorneys' fees.

(2) Nothing in this section precludes the right to commence action in a court under chapter 12.40 RCW for small claims. [1995 c 187 §1; 1993 c 229 §67; 1991 c 168 §1; 1986 c 128 §1; 1981 c 254 §1; 1969 c 62 §1; 1967 ex.s. c 23 §1.]

NOTES: Recovery of attorneys' fees—Effective date—1993 c 229: See RCW 62A.11-111 and 62A.11-112. Savings—Severability—1967 ex.s. c 23: See notes following RCW 19.52.005.

RCW 62A.3-520 Statutory form for notice of dishonor. The notice of dishonor shall be sent by mail to the drawer at the drawer's last known address, and the notice shall be substantially in the following form:

NOTICE OF DISHONOR OF CHECK

A check drawn by you and made payable by you to _____ in the amount of _____ has not been accepted for payment by _____, which is the drawee bank designated on your check. This check is dated _____, and it is numbered, No._____.

You are CAUTIONED that unless you pay the amount of this check within fifteen days after the date this letter is postmarked, you may very well have to pay the following additional amounts:

(1) Costs of collecting the amount of the check, including an attorney's fee which will be set by the court;

(2) Interest on the amount of the check which shall accrue at the rate of twelve percent per annum from the date of dishonor; and

(3) Three hundred dollars or three times the face amount of the check, whichever is less, by award of the court.

You are also CAUTIONED that law enforcement agencies may be provided with a copy of this notice of dishonor and the check drawn by you for the possibility of proceeding with criminal charges if you do not pay the amount of this check within fifteen days after the date this letter is postmarked.

You are advised to make your payment to _____ at the following address:_____

[1993 c 229 §68; 1991 c 168 §2; 1986 c 128 §2; 1981 c 254 §2; 1969 c 62 §2.]

NOTES: Recovery of attorneys' fees—Effective date—1993 c 229: See RCW 62A.11-111 and 62A.11-112.

RCW 62A.3-522 Notice of dishonor—Affidavit of service by mail. In addition to sending a notice of dishonor to the drawer of the check under RCW 62A.3-520, the holder of the check shall execute an affidavit certifying service of the notice by mail. The affidavit of service by mail must be attached to a copy of the notice of dishonor and must be substantially in the following form:

AFFIDAVIT OF SERVICE BY MAIL

I, _____, hereby certify that on the _____ day of _____, 20____, a copy of the foregoing Notice was served on _____ by mailing via the United States Postal Service, postage prepaid, at _____, Washington.

Dated: _____

_____ (Signature)

The holder shall retain the affidavit with the check but shall file a copy of the affidavit with the clerk of the court in which an action on the check is commenced. [1993 c 229 §69; 1981 c 254 §3.]

NOTES: Recovery of attorneys' fees—Effective date—1993 c 229: See RCW 62A.11-111 and 62A.11-112.

RCW 62A.3-525 Consequences for failing to comply with requirements. No interest, collection costs, and attorneys' fees, except handling fees, are recoverable on any dishonored check under the provisions of RCW 62A.3-515 where the holder of the check or any agent, employee, or assign of the holder has demanded:

(1) Interest or collection costs in excess of that provided by RCW 62A.3-515; or

(2) Interest or collection costs prior to the expiration of fifteen days after the mailing of notice of dishonor, as provided by RCW 62A.3-515 and 62A.3-520; or

(3) Attorneys' fees either without having the fees set by the court, or prior to the expiration of fifteen days after the mailing of notice of dishonor, as provided by RCW 62A.3-515 and 62A.3-520. [1993 c 229 §70; 1981 c 254 §4; 1969 c 62 §3.]

NOTES: Recovery of attorneys' fees—Effective date—1993 c 229: See RCW 62A.11-111 and 62A.11-112.

TITLE 64. REAL PROPERTY AND CONVEYANCES
Chapter 64.08 Acknowledgments.

RCW 64.08.010 Who may take acknowledgments. Acknowledgments of deeds, mortgages and other instruments in writing, required to be acknowledged may be taken in this state before a justice of the supreme court, or the clerk thereof, or the deputy of such clerk, before a judge of the court of appeals, or the clerk thereof, before a judge of the superior court, or qualified court commissioner thereof, or the clerk thereof, or the deputy of such clerk, or a county auditor, or the deputy of such auditor, or a qualified notary public, or a qualified United States commissioner appointed by any district court of the United States for this state, and all said instruments heretofore executed and acknowledged according to the provisions of this section are hereby declared legal and valid. [1971 c 81 §131; 1931 c 13 §1; 1929 c 33 §3; RRS §10559. Prior: 1913 c 14 §1; Code 1881 §2315; 1879 p 110 §1; 1877 p 317 §5; 1875 p 107 §1; 1873 p 466 §5.]

RCW 64.08.020 Acknowledgments out of state—Certificate. Acknowledgments of deeds conveying or encumbering real estate situated in this state, or any interest therein, and other instruments in writing, required to be acknowledged, may be taken in any other state or territory of the United States, the District of Columbia, or in any possession of the United States, before any person authorized to take the acknowledgments of deeds by the laws of the state, territory, district or possession wherein the acknowledgment is taken, or before any commissioner appointed by the governor of this state, for that purpose, but unless such acknowledgment is taken before a commissioner so appointed by the governor, or before the clerk of a court of record of such state, territory, district or possession, or before a notary public or other officer having a seal of office, the instrument shall have attached thereto a certificate of the clerk of a court of record of the county, parish, or other political subdivision of such state, territory, district or possession wherein the acknowledgment was taken, under the seal of said court, certifying that the person who took the acknowledgment, and whose name is subscribed to the certificate thereof, was at the date thereof such officer as here presented himself to be, authorized by law to take acknowledgments of deeds, and that the clerk verily believes the signature of the person subscribed to the certificate of acknowledgment to be genuine. [1929 c 33 §4; RRS §§10560, 10561. Prior: Code 1881 §§2316, 2317; 1877 p 313 §§6, 7; 1873 p 466 §§6, 7; 1867 pp 93, 94 §§1, 2; 1866 p 89 §1; 1865 p 25 §1. Formerly RCW 64.08.020 and 64.08.030.]

RCW 64.08.040 Foreign acknowledgments, who may take.
Acknowledgments of deeds conveying or encumbering real estate situated in this state, or any interest therein and other instruments in writing, required to be acknowledged, may be taken in any foreign country before any minister, plenipotentiary, secretary of legation, charge d'affaires, consul general, consul, vice consul, consular agent, or commercial agent appointed by the United States government, or before any notary public, or before the judge, clerk, or other proper officer of any court of said country, or before the mayor or other chief magistrate of any city, town or other municipal corporation therein. [1929 c 33 §5; RRS §10563, part. Prior: 1901 c 53 §1; 1888 p 1 §1; Code 1881 §2319; 1875 p 108 §2.]

RCW 64.08.050 Certificate of acknowledgment—Evidence. The officer, or person, taking an acknowledgment as in this chapter provided, shall certify the same by a certificate written upon or annexed to the instrument acknowledged and signed by him or her and sealed with his or her official seal, if any, and reciting in substance that the person, or persons, known to him or her as, or determined by satisfactory evidence to be, the person, or persons, whose name, or names, are signed to the instrument as executing the same, acknowledged before him or her on the date stated in the certificate that he, she, or they, executed the same freely and voluntarily. Such certificate shall be prima facie evidence of the facts therein recited. The officer or person taking the acknowledgment has satisfactory evidence that a person is the person whose name is signed on the instrument if that person: (1) Is personally known to the officer or person taking the acknowledgment; (2) is identified upon the oath or affirmation of a credible witness personally known to the officer or person taking the acknowledgment; or (3) is identified on the basis of identification documents. [1988 c 69 §1; 1929 c 33 §6; RRS §§10564, 10565. Prior: Code 1881 §§2320, 2321; 1879 p 158 §§2,3.]

RCW 64.08.060 Form of certificate for individual. A certificate of acknowledgment for an individual, substantially in the following form or, after December 31, 1985, substantially in the form set forth in RCW 42.44.100(1), shall be sufficient for the purposes of this chapter and for any acknowledgment required to betaken in accordance with this chapter:

State of _____ ss.
County of _____
    On this day personally appeared before me (here insert the name
of grantor or grantors) to me known to be the individual, or
individuals described in and who executed the within and foregoing
instrument, and acknowledged that he (she or they) signed the same
as his (her or their) free and voluntary act and deed, for the uses and
purposes therein mentioned. Given under my hand and official seal
this _____ day of _____, 20_____
(Signature of officer and official seal)

   If acknowledgment is taken before a notary public of this state the signature
shall be followed by substantially the following: Notary Public in and for the
state of Washington, residing at _____, (giving place of residence).
[1988c 69 §2; 1929 c 33 §13; RRS §10566. Prior: 1888 p 51 §2; 1886 p 179 §7.]

   RCW 64.08.070 Form of certificate for corporation. A certificate of
acknowledgment for a corporation, substantially in the following form or, after
December 31, 1985, substantially in the form set forth in RCW 42.44.100(2), shall
be sufficient for the purposes of this chapter and for any acknowledgment
required to betaken in accordance with this chapter:

State of _____ ss.
County of _____
    On this _____ day of _____, 19____, before me personally
appeared _____, to me known to be the (president, vice
president, secretary, treasurer, or other authorized officer or agent, as
the case may be) of the corporation that executed the within and
foregoing instrument, and acknowledged said instrument to be the free
and voluntary act and deed of said corporation, for the uses and
purposes therein mentioned, and on oath stated that he was
authorized to execute said instrument and that the seal affixed is the
corporate seal of said corporation.
    In Witness Whereof I have hereunto set my hand and affixed my
official seal the day and year first above written. (Signature and title
of officer with place of residence of notary public.)

   [1988 c 69 §3; 1929 c 33 §14; RRS §10567. Prior: 1903 c 132 §1.]

   **RCW 64.08.090 Authority of superintendents, business managers and
officers of correctional institutions to take acknowledgments and
administer oaths—Procedure.** The superintendents, associate and assistant
superintendents, business managers, records officers and camp superintendents
of any correctional institution or facility operated by the state of Washington are
hereby authorized and empowered to take acknowledgments on any instruments
of writing, and certify the same in the manner required by law, and to administer
all oaths required by law to be administered, all of the foregoing acts to have the
same effect as if performed by a notary public: PROVIDED, That such authority
shall only extend to taking acknowledgments for and administering oaths to
officers, employees and residents of such institutions and facilities. None of the
individuals herein empowered to take acknowledgments and administer oaths
shall demand or accept any fee or compensation whatsoever for administering
or taking any oath, affirmation, or acknowledgment under the authority conferred

by this section.

In certifying any oath or in signing any instrument officially, an individual empowered to do so under this section shall, in addition to his name, state in writing his place of residence, the date of his action, and affix the seal of the institution where he is employed: PROVIDED, That in certifying any oath to be used in any of the courts of this state, it shall not be necessary to append an impression of the official seal of the institution. [1972 ex.s. c 58 §1.]

RCW 64.08.100 Acknowledgments by persons unable to sign name. Any person who is otherwise competent but is physically unable to sign his or her name or make a mark may make an acknowledgment authorized under this chapter by orally directing the notary public or other authorized officer taking the acknowledgment to sign the person's name on his or her behalf. In taking an acknowledgment under this section, the notary public or other authorized officer shall, in addition to stating his or her name and place of residence, state that the signature in the acknowledgment was obtained under the authority of this section. [1987 c 76 §2.]

TITLE 65. RECORDING, REGISTRATION, AND LEGAL PUBLICATION

Editor's Note: This new law is not yet codified within Title 65.

NEW SECTION. Sec. 1 This chapter may be known and cited as the uniform real property electronic recording act.

NEW SECTION. Sec. 2 The definitions in this section apply throughout this chapter unless the context clearly requires otherwise.
  (1) "Document" means information that is:
  (a) Inscribed on a tangible medium or that is stored in an electronic or other medium, and is retrievable in perceivable form; and
  (b) Eligible to be recorded in the land records maintained by the recording officer.
  (2) "Electronic" means relating to technology having electrical, digital, magnetic, wireless, optical, electromagnetic, or similar capabilities.
  (3) "Electronic document" means a document that is received by the recording officer in an electronic form.
  (4) "Electronic signature" means an electronic sound, symbol, or process attached to or logically associated with a document and executed or adopted by a person with the intent to sign the document.
  (5) "Person" means an individual, corporation, business trust, estate, trust, partnership, limited liability company, association, joint venture, public corporation, government, or governmental subdivision, agency, or instrumentality, or any other legal or commercial entity.
  (6) "State" means a state of the United States, the District of Columbia, Puerto Rico, the United States Virgin Islands, or any territory or insular possession subject to the jurisdiction of the United States.
  (7) "E-recording standards commission" means the body of stakeholders appointed by the secretary of state to review electronic recording standards and make recommendations to the secretary under section 5 of this act.

NEW SECTION. Sec. 3 (1) If a law requires, as a condition for recording, that a document be an original, be on paper or another tangible medium, or be in writing, the requirement is satisfied by an electronic document satisfying this chapter.
  (2) If a law requires, as a condition for recording, that a document be signed,

the requirement is satisfied by an electronic signature.

(3) A requirement that a document or a signature associated with a document be notarized, acknowledged, verified, witnessed, or made under oath is satisfied if the electronic signature of the person authorized to perform that act, and all other information required to be included, is attached to or logically associated with the document or signature. A physical or electronic image of a stamp, impression, or seal need not accompany an electronic signature.

NEW SECTION. Sec. 4 (1) In this section, "paper document" means a document that is received by the recording officer in a form that is not electronic.

(2) A recording officer:

(a) Who performs any of the functions listed in this section shall do so in compliance with the rules adopted by the secretary of state for the electronic recording of documents;

(b) May receive, index, store, archive, and transmit electronic documents;

(c) May provide for access to, and for search and retrieval of, documents and information by electronic means;

(d) Who accepts electronic documents for recording shall continue to accept paper documents as authorized by state law and shall place entries for both types of documents in the same index;

(e) May convert paper documents accepted for recording into electronic form;

(f) May convert information previously recorded into electronic form;

(g) May, after receiving approval pursuant to RCW 36.29.190, accept electronically any fee or tax that the recording officer is authorized to collect;

(h) May agree with other officials of a state, or a political subdivision thereof, or of the United States, on procedures or processes to facilitate the electronic satisfaction of prior approvals and conditions precedent to recording and the electronic payment of fees or taxes.

NEW SECTION. Sec. 5 The office of the secretary of state shall create and appoint an e-recording standards commission. The e-recording standards commission shall review electronic recording standards and make recommendations to the secretary of state for rules necessary to implement this chapter. A majority of the commission must be county recorders or auditors. The commission may include assessors, treasurers, land title company representatives, escrow agents, and mortgage brokers, the state archivist, and any other party the secretary of state deems appropriate. The term of the commissioners will be set by the secretary of state.

To keep the standards and practices of recording officers in this state in harmony with the standards and practices of recording offices in other jurisdictions that enact this chapter and to keep the technology used by recording officers in this state compatible with technology used by recording offices in other jurisdictions that enact this chapter, the office of the secretary of state, so far as is consistent with the purposes, policies, and provisions of this chapter, in adopting, amending, and repealing standards shall consider:

(1) The standards and practices of other jurisdictions;

(2) The most recent standards adopted by national standard-setting bodies, such as the property records industry association;

(3) The views of interested persons and governmental officials and entities;

(4) The needs of counties of varying size, population, and resources; and

(5) Standards requiring adequate information security protection to ensure

that electronic documents are accurate, authentic, adequately preserved, and resistant to tampering.

NEW SECTION. Sec. 6 In applying and construing this chapter, consideration must be given to the need to promote uniformity of the law with respect to its subject matter among states that enact a uniform real property electronic recording act.

NEW SECTION. Sec. 7 This chapter modifies, limits, and supersedes the federal electronic signatures in global and national commerce act (15 U.S.C. Sec. 7001, et seq.) but does not modify, limit, or supersede section 101(c) of that act or authorize electronic delivery of any of the notices described in section 103(b) of that act.

NEW SECTION. Sec. 8 Sections 1 through 7 of this act constitute a new chapter in Title 65 RCW

Chapter 65.04 Duties of county auditor.

RCW 65.04.045 Recorded instruments—Requirements—Form. (1) When any instrument is presented to a county auditor or recording officer for recording, the first page of the instrument shall contain:

(a) A top margin of at least three inches and a one-inch margin on the bottom and sides, except that an instrument may be recorded if a minor portion of a notary seal, incidental writing, or minor portion of a signature extends beyond the margins;

(b) The top left-hand side of the page shall contain the name and address to whom the instrument will be returned;

(c) The title or titles, or type or types, of the instrument to be recorded indicating the kind or kinds of documents or transactions contained therein immediately below the three-inch margin at the top of the page. The auditor or recording officer shall be required to index only the title or titles captioned on the document;

(d) Reference numbers of documents assigned or released with reference to the document page number where additional references can be found, if applicable;

(e) The names of the grantor(s) and grantee(s), as defined under RCW 65.04.015, with reference to the document page number where additional names are located, if applicable;

(f) An abbreviated legal description of the property, and for purposes of this subsection, "abbreviated legal description of the property" means lot, block, plat, or section, township, range, and quarter/quarter section, and reference to the document page number where the full legal description is included, if applicable;

(g) The assessor's property tax parcel or account number set forth separately from the legal description or other text.

(2) All pages of the document shall be on sheets of paper of a weight and color capable of producing a legible image that are not larger than fourteen inches long and eight and one-half inches wide with text printed or written in eight point type or larger. All text within the document must be of sufficient color and clarity to ensure that when the text is imaged all text is readable. Further, all pages presented for recording must have at minimum a one-inch margin on the top, bottom, and sides for all pages except page one, except that an instrument may be recorded if a minor

portion of a notary seal, incidental writing, or minor portion of a signature extends beyond the margins, be prepared in ink color capable of being imaged, and have all seals legible and capable of being imaged.

No attachments, except firmly attached bar code or address labels, may be affixed to the pages. ...

Washington Administrative Code
Chapter 308-30
NOTARIES PUBLIC

Section
308-30-005   Mailing address.
308-30-010   Size and form of notary seal or stamp.
308-30-020   Maximum fees that may be charged by notaries public.
308-30-030   Applications for appointment as notary public.
308-30-040   Resignation or revocation of notary appointment.
308-30-050   Replacement of lost or stolen notary seals or stamps.
308-30-060   Department to be notified of change of name or address.
308-30-070   Requests for evidence of authenticity.
308-30-080   Appeals of denials and revocations of notary appointments.
308-30-090   Forms.
308-30-100   Fees.
308-30-120   Notary signature.
308-30-130   Expired stamp or seal.
308-30-140   Notification of legal actions.
308-30-150   Continuous qualification required.
308-30-155   Satisfactory evidence of identity.
308-30-160   Testimonials.
308-30-170   Application of brief adjudicative proceedings.
308-30-180   Preliminary record in brief adjudicative proceedings.
308-30-190   Conduct of brief adjudicative proceedings.

WAC 308-30-005 Mailing address. All correspondence is to be directed to the Department of Licensing, Notary Public Section, Post Office Box 9048 (in person 405 Black Lake Bl. S.W.) Olympia, Washington 98507-9048. [Statutory Authority: RCW 42.44.190. 93-05-009, §308-30-005, filed 2/5/93, effective 3/8/93.]

WAC 308-30-010 Size and form of notary seal or stamp. A notary seal shall be one and five-eighths inches minimum in diameter. If a notary stamp is used the following requirements shall apply:
(1) The type shall be a minimum of 8 point type.
(2) The stamp shall be minimum one and five-eighths inches in diameter. If a rectangular stamp is used the minimum dimensions shall be one inch wide by one and five-eighths inches long.
(3) The imprint shall be affixed with indelible ink only.
(4) The face of any notary stamp shall contain permanently affixed letters and numerals and shall not be preprinted.
(5) The use of the Washington state seal on the notary stamp or seal is prohibited.
(6) A vendor may not provide a notarial seal, or stamp, either inking or embossing, to a person claiming to be a notary, unless the person presents a photo copy of the person's Notary Certificate.
(7) A notary applying for a seal or stamp as a result of a name change shall present a copy to the vendor of the certificate evidencing the notary's

name change from the director. [Statutory Authority: RCW 42.44.190. 93-05-009, §308-30-010, filed 2/5/93, effective 3/8/93. Statutory Authority: 1985 c 156 §§ 5 and 20. 85-24-025 (Order PL 571), §308-30-010, filed 11/26/85, effective 1/1/86.]

WAC 308-30-020 What fees may a notary public charge? (1) The maximum fees a notary may charge for notarial acts are:

Notarial Act	Fee
Witnessing or attesting a signature	$10.00
Taking acknowledgement or verification upon oath or affirmation	$10.00
Certifying or attesting a copy	$10.00
Receiving or noting a protest of a negotiable instrument	$10.00
Being present at demand, tender, or deposit, and noting the same	$10.00
Administering an oath or affirmation	$10.00
Certifying that an event has occurred or an act has been performed	$10.00

(2) A notary public need not charge for notarial acts. A notary who chooses to charge for notarial acts shall conspicuously display in their place of business, or present to each customer outside their business, an English-language schedule of fees for notarial acts. No part of the displayed notarial fee schedule may be printed in smaller than 10-point type.

(3) A notary may charge actual costs of copying any instrument or record.

(4) A notary may charge a travel fee when traveling to perform a notarial act if:

(a) The notary and the person requesting the notarial act agree upon the travel fee in advance of the travel; and

(b) The notary explains to the person requesting the notarial act that the travel fee is in addition to the notarial fee in subsection (1) of this section and is not required by law.

WAC 308-30-030 Applications for appointment as notary public.
Applications for appointment as notary public may be obtained from the department of licensing. Every application submitted for appointment as a notary public must be accompanied by the required surety bond and the prescribed fee and shall in all ways comply with the requirements of chapter 42.44 RCW. [Statutory Authority: RCW 42.44.190. 93-05-009, §308-30-030, filed 2/5/93, effective 3/8/93. Statutory Authority: 1985 c 156 §§5 and 20. 85-24-025 (Order PL 571), §308-30-030, filed 11/26/85, effective 1/1/86.]

WAC 308-30-040 Resignation or revocation of notary appointment.
Voluntary resignation by a notary public shall be submitted in writing to the department of licensing. If a notary public voluntarily resigns his or her notary appointment or if the notary appointment is revoked, suspended or restricted, the notary public must mail or deliver his or her notary stamp or seal to the department of licensing. No voluntary resignation of a notary appointment shall be effective until the notary seal or stamp is mailed or delivered to the notary section. [Statutory Authority: RCW 42.44.190. 93-05-009, §308-30-040, filed 2/5/93, effective 3/8/93. Statutory Authority: 1985 c 156 §§5 and 20. 85-24-025 (Order PL 571), §308-30-040, filed 11/26/85, effective 1/1/86.]

WAC 308-30-050 Replacement of lost or stolen notary seals or stamps. When a notary seal or stamp is lost or stolen the department of licensing is to be notified by certified mail. The notice must set forth the fact that the notary seal or stamp has been lost or stolen and be signed by the notary public. The notary public may then obtain a replacement notary seal or stamp. The new notary seal or stamp must contain some variance from the original seal or stamp. If the lost or stolen notary seal or stamp is found or recovered after a replacement has been obtained the original seal or stamp shall be surrendered to the department of licensing. [Statutory Authority: RCW 42.44.190. 93-05-009, §308-30-050, filed 2/5/93, effective 3/8/93. Statutory Authority: 1985 c 156 §§5 and 20. 85-24-025 (Order PL 571), §308-30-050, filed 11/26/85, effective 1/1/86.]

WAC 308-30-060 Department to be notified of change of name or address. When a notary public changes his or her name or address, the department of licensing must be notified in writing of such name and/or address change. The notification of name change must be accompanied by a bond rider from the bonding company amending the notary bond, and the prescribed fee for a name change which provides a duplicate notary certificate showing the new name. There is no charge for an address change. [Statutory Authority: RCW 42.44.190. 93-05-009, § 308-30-060, filed 2/5/93, effective 3/8/93. Statutory Authority: 1985 c 156 §§5 and 20. 85-24-025 (Order PL 571), §308-30-060, filed 11/26/85, effective 1/1/86.]

WAC 308-30-070 Requests for evidence of authenticity. Requests for evidences of authenticity of notarial commission must be in writing, accompanied by the prescribed fee, the original document, and mailed to the department of licensing. [Statutory Authority: RCW 42.44.190. 93-05-009, §308-30-070, filed 2/5/93, effective 3/8/93. Statutory Authority: 1985 c 156 §§5 and 20. 85-24-025 (Order PL 571), §308-30-070, filed 11/26/85, effective 1/1/86.]

WAC 308-30-080 Appeals of denials and revocations of notary appointments. Notices of appeals of denials and revocations of notary appointments must be in writing and mailed or delivered to the department of licensing. The written notification of appeal must be received by the department within twenty days of the date of denial or revocation or the right to appeal is waived. When the notification of appeal is mailed, the postmarked date will be accepted as the date of receipt by the department of licensing. Procedures on appeal will be as provided in the Administrative Procedure Act, chapter 34.05 RCW, and rules adopted thereunder. [Statutory Authority: RCW 42.44.190.93-05-009, §308-30-080, filed 2/5/93, effective 3/8/93. Statutory Authority: 1985 c 156 §§5 and 20. 85-24-025 (Order PL 571), §308-30-080, filed 11/26/85, effective 1/1/86.]

WAC 308-30-090 Forms. (1) The forms in RCW 42.44.100 are only suggested certificates with the sufficient information included. These forms may be used; however, when a specific form is required by a specific statute, the required form shall be used.

(2) A nonattorney notary may complete notarial certificates, and may not assist another person in drafting, completing, selecting, or understanding a document or transaction requiring a notarial act. This does not preclude a notary who is duly qualified in a particular profession from giving advice relating to matters in that professional field. [Statutory Authority: RCW 42.44.190. 93-05-009, §308-30-090, filed 2/5/93, effective 3/8/93. Statutory Authority: 1985 c 156 §§5 and 20. 85-24-025 (Order PL 571), §308-30-090, filed 11/26/85, effective 1/1/86.]

WAC 308-30-100 Fees. The following fees shall be charged by the director of the department of licensing:

Title of Fee	Fee
Application for notary appointment	$30.00
Renewal of notary appointment	$30.00
Duplicate certificate of appointment (including change of name)	$15.00
Evidence of verification of notarial commission	$15.00
Apostille	$15.00

[Statutory Authority: RCW 42.44.190, 43.35.055, 43.24.086, WAC 308-30-100. 05-12-047, § 308-30-100, filed 5/26/05, effective 6/26/05. Statutory Authority: RCW 43.24.086. 90-06-052, § 308-30-100, filed 3/2/90, effective 4/2/90. Statutory Authority: 1985 c 156 §§ 5 and 20. 85-24-025 (Order PL 571), § 308-30-100, filed 11/26/85, effective 1/1/86.]

WAC 308-30-120 Notary signature. Upon completion of a notarial act, the notary must sign the notary certification using his/her name exactly as it appears on the notary certificate of appointment and the stamp or seal. The notary's name must be legibly printed or stamped directly below their signature. [Statutory Authority: RCW 42.44.190. 93-05-009, §308-30-120, filed 2/5/93, effective 3/8/93.]

WAC 308-30-130 Expired stamp or seal. The use of a stamp or seal with an expired date is prohibited. [Statutory Authority: RCW 42.44.190. 93-05-009, §308-30-130, filed 2/5/93, effective 3/8/93.]

WAC 308-30-140 Notification of legal actions. The notary must notify the department of licensing of any conviction against him or her of official misconduct, and/or civil or criminal charges. Notification must be submitted within thirty days of such happening. [Statutory Authority: RCW 42.44.190. 93-05-009, §308-30-140, filed 2/5/93, effective 3/8/93.]

WAC 308-30-150 Continuous qualification required. A notary public must continue to meet the requirements of RCW 42.44.020 (1)(b) or (c) throughout the term of appointment. A notary who fails to meet any one or more of the aforementioned requirements shall resign, or the director shall institute hearings to determine if the requirements have been met by the notary. [Statutory Authority: RCW 42.44.190. 93-05-009, §308-30-150, filed 2/5/93, effective 3/8/93.]

WAC 308-30-155 Satisfactory evidence of identity. Satisfactory evidence of an individual identity shall be based on one of the following:
(1) Current documents issued by a federal or state government with the individual's photograph, signature, and physical description.
(2) The oath or affirmation of a credible person who personally knows the individual. [Statutory Authority: RCW 42.44.190. 93-05-009, §308-30-155, filed 2/5/93, effective 3/8/93.]

WAC 308-30-160 Testimonials. A notary may not endorse or promote any service, contest, or other offering if the notary's seal or title is used in the endorsement or promotional statement. [Statutory Authority: RCW 42.44.190. 93-05-009, §308-30-160, filed 2/5/93, effective 3/8/93.]

WAC 308-30-170 Application of brief adjudicative proceedings. The director adopts RCW 34.05.482 through 34.05.494 for the administration of brief adjudicative proceedings conducted by request, and/or at the discretion of the director pursuant to RCW 34.05.482, for the categories of matters set forth below. Brief adjudicative proceedings will be limited to a determination of one or more of the following issues:

(1) Whether an applicant for an appointment meets the minimum criteria for an appointment as a notary public in this state and the department proposes to deny the application;

(2) Whether a person is in compliance with the terms and conditions of a final order or agreement previously issued by the department; and

(3) Whether an appointment holder requesting renewal has submitted all required information and whether an appointment holder meets minimum criteria for renewal. [Statutory Authority: RCW 34.05.410 (1)(a) and 34.05.482 (1)(c). 97-10-052, §308-30-170, filed 5/1/97, effective 6/1/97.]

WAC 308-30-180 Preliminary record in brief adjudicative proceedings.
(1) The preliminary record with respect to an application for appointment or reappointment shall consist of:

(a) The application for appointment or reappointment and all associated documents;

(b) All documents relied upon by the director in proposing to deny the appointment or reappointment; and

(c) All correspondence between the applicant for appointment or reappointment and the director regarding the application.

(2) The preliminary record with respect to determination of compliance with a previously issued final order or agreement shall consist of:

(a) The previously issued final order or agreement;

(b) All reports or other documents submitted by, or at the direction of, the appointment holder, in full or partial fulfillment of the terms of the final order or agreement;

(c) All correspondence between the appointment holder and the director regarding compliance with the final order or agreement; and

(d) All documents relied upon by the director showing that the appointment holder has failed to comply with the previously issued final order or agreement. [Statutory Authority: RCW 34.05.410 (1)(a) and 34.05.482 (1)(c). 97-10-052, §308-30-180, filed 5/1/97, effective 6/1/97.]

WAC 308-30-190 Conduct of brief adjudicative proceedings. (1) Brief adjudicative proceedings shall be conducted by a presiding officer for brief adjudicative proceedings designated by the director. The presiding officer for brief adjudicative proceedings shall not have personally participated in the decision which resulted in the request for a brief adjudicative proceeding.

(2) The parties or their representatives may present written documentation. The presiding officer for brief adjudicative proceedings shall designate the date by which written documents must be submitted by the parties.

(3) The presiding officer for brief adjudicative proceedings may, in his or her discretion, entertain oral argument from the parties or their representatives.

(4) No witnesses may appear to testify.

(5) In addition to the record, the presiding officer for brief adjudicative proceedings may employ department expertise as a basis for the decision.

(6) The presiding officer for brief adjudicative proceedings shall not issue an oral order. Within ten days of the final date for submission of materials or oral argument, if any, the presiding officer for brief adjudicative proceedings shall enter an initial order. [Statutory Authority: RCW 34.05.410 (1)(a) and 34.05.482 (1)(c). 97-10-052, §308-30-190, filed 5/1/97, effective 6/1/97.] ∎

Office of the Washington Dept. of Licensing

Department of Licensing
Notaries Public Licensing Program

Walk-in Address:
405 Black Lake Bl. S.W.
Olympia, WA 98507

Mailing Address:
P.O. Box 9048
Olympia, WA 98507-9048

Telephone: (360) 664-1550
Fax: (360) 586-4414

   In addition, there are many useful resources available at the state's official Web site, including links to legislative information, the Secretary of State's office and research bureaus. You can access the state's home page at www.secstate.wa.gov.

   Information for Notaries appears at the Department of Licensing's Notary page at www.dol.wa.gov/unfc/notfront.htm.

Bureaus of Vital Statistics

Washington Notaries are strongly discouraged from making certified copies of any document that is either recordable or a public record. Persons requesting notarization, certification, or certified copies of birth or death certificates should be referred to the appropriate public office. The following state agencies can provide certified copies of birth and death records of persons who were born or have died in the respective states, as can certain local offices not listed here:

Alabama
Vital Records
Department of Public Health
P.O. Box 5625
Montgomery, AL 36103-5625

Alaska
Bureau of Vital Statistics
Dept. of Health & Social Services
5441 Commercial Bl.
Juneau, AK 99801

Arizona
Office of Vital Records
Dept. of Health Services
P.O. Box 3887
Phoenix, AZ 85030-3887

Arkansas
Division of Vital Records
Department of Health
4815 West Markham Street, Slot 44
Little Rock, AR 72205-3867

California
Office of Vital Records
Department of Health Services
P.O. Box 997410, MS: 5103
Sacramento, CA 95899-7410

Colorado
Health Statistics
Department of Health
CHEIS-HS-A1
4300 Cherry Creek Drive South
Denver, CO 80246-1530

Connecticut
CT Department of Public Health
State Office of Vital Records
410 Capitol Ave., MS#11VRS
P.O. Box 340308
Hartford, CT 06134-0308

Delaware
Delaware Health Statistics Center
Office of Vital Statistics
Jesse S. Cooper Building
417 Federal Street
Dover, DE 19901

District of Columbia
Department of Health
John A. Wilson Building
1350 Pennsylvania Avenue NW
Washington, DC 20004

Florida
Department of Health
Office of Vital Statistics
4052 Bald Cypress Way
Tallahassee, FL 32399-1701

Georgia
Vital Records
2600 Skyland Drive NE
Atlanta, GA 30319-3640

Hawaii
State Department of Health
Vital Statistics Section
P.O. Box 3378
Honolulu, HI 96801

Idaho
Department of Health and Welfare
Vital Statistics Unit
450 West State Street, 1st Floor
P.O. Box 83720
Boise, ID 83720

Illinois
Health Statistics
Department of Public Health
605 West Jefferson Street
Springfield, IL 62702-5097

Indiana
Vital Records Department
Indiana State Department of Health
6 West Washington Street
Indianapolis, IN 46204

Iowa
Department of Public Health
Bureau of Vital Records
Lucas Office Building, 1st Floor
321 East 12th Street
Des Moines, IA 50319-0075

Kansas
Office of Vital Statistics
1000 SW Jackson Street, Suite 120
Topeka, KS 66612

Kentucky
Office of Vital Statistics
Department for Health Services
275 East Main Street-1E-A
Frankfort, KY 40621-0001

Louisiana
Vital Records Registry
P.O. Box 60630
New Orleans, LA 70160

Maine
Department of Human Services
Vital Records
221 State Street, Station 11
11 State House Station
Augusta, ME 04333-0011

Maryland
Division of Vital Records
6550 Reisterstown Plaza
Reisterstown Road Plaza
Baltimore, MD 21215

Massachusetts
Vital Records and Statistics
150 Mt. Vernon Street, First Floor
Dorchester, MA 02125-3105

Michigan
Department of Community Health
3423 N. Martin Luther King Blvd.
P.O. Box 30721
Lansing, MI 48909

Minnesota
Minnesota Department of Health
Attention: Office of the State Registrar
P.O. Box 64882
St. Paul, MN 55164-0882

Mississippi
Vital Records
571 Stadium Drive
P.O. Box 1700
Jackson, MS 39215-1700

Missouri
Department of Health
Bureau of Vital Records
930 Wildwood
P.O. Box 570
Jefferson City, MO 65102

Montana
Office of Vital Statistics
Department of Public Health
P.O. Box 4210
111 North Sanders, Room 209
Helena, MT 59604

Nebraska
Vital Statistics
Department of Health
P.O. Box 95044
Lincoln, NE 68509-5044

Nevada
Office of Vital Records
4150 Technology Way, Suite 104
Carson City, Nevada 89706

New Hampshire
NH Department of State
Division of Vital Records
Administration
71 South Fruit Street
Concord, NH 03301-2410

New Jersey
Vital Statistics
Customer Service Unit
P.O. Box 370
Trenton, NJ 08625-0370

New Mexico
Vital Records and Health Statistics
P.O. Box 26110
1105 St. Francis Drive
Santa Fe, NM 87502

New York
New York State Department of
Health
Vital Records Section
Certification Unit
P.O. Box 2602
Albany, NY 12220-2602

New York City
Office of Vital Records
NYC Department of Health and
Mental Hygiene
125 Worth Street, CN4, Room 133
New York, NY 10013-4090

North Carolina
Vital Records
1903 Mail Service Center
Raleigh, NC 27699-1903

North Dakota
Division of Vital Records
600 East Boulevard Ave.
Department 301
Bismarck, ND 58505-0200

Ohio
Ohio Department of Health
Vital Statistics
P.O. Box 15098
Columbus, OH 43215-0098

Oklahoma
Vital Records Service
State Department of Health
1000 Northeast Tenth, Room 111
Oklahoma City, OK 73117

Oregon
Oregon Vital Records
800 NE Oregon Street, Ste 205
P.O. Box 14050
Portland, OR 97293

Pennsylvania
Vital Records
State Department of Health
101 S. Mercer Street
P.O. Box 1528
New Castle, PA 16101

Rhode Island
Office of Vital Records
Department of Health
3 Capitol Hill
Room 101
Providence, RI 02908-5097

South Carolina
Office of Vital Records
2600 Bull Street
Columbia, SC 29201

South Dakota
Vital Records
207 E. Missouri Ave., Suite #1A
Pierre, SD 57501

Tennessee
Vital Records
Central Services Building
1st Floor
421 5th Avenue North
Nashville, TN 37247

Texas
Bureau of Vital Statistics
Department of Health
P.O. Box 12040
Austin, TX 78711-2040

Utah
Vital Records & Statistics
Cannon Health Building
288 North 1460 West
P.O. Box 141012
Salt Lake City, UT 84114-1012

Vermont
Department of Health
Vital Records Section
108 Cherry Street
P.O. Box 70
Burlington, VT 05402-0070

Virginia
Office of Vital Records
P.O. Box 1000
Richmond, VA 23218

Washington
Department of Health
Center for Health Statistics
P.O. Box 9709
Olympia, WA 98507-9709

West Virginia
Vital Registration Office
350 Capitol Street, Room 165
Charleston, WV 25301-3701

Wisconsin
Vital Records
1 West Wilson Street
P.O. Box 309
Madison, WI 53701-0309

Wyoming
Vital Records Services
Hathaway Building
Cheyenne, WY 82002

American Samoa
American Samoa Office of
Records and Vital Statistics
LBJ Tropical Medical Center
Department of Health Services
American Samoa Government
Pago Pago, AS 96799

Guam
Department of Public Health and
Social Services
Government of Guam
P.O. Box 2816
Agana, GU M.I. 96932

Northern Mariana Islands
Bureau of Health Planning
Vital Statistics Office
P.O. Box 500409 CK
Saipan, MP 96950-0409

Panama Canal Zone
Vital Records Section
Passport Services
U.S. Department of State
1111 19th Street NW, Suite 510
Washington, DC, CZ 34011-2300

Puerto Rico
Department of Health
Demographic Registry
P.O. Box 11854
Fernández Juncos Station
San Juan, PR 00910

Virgin Islands (St. Croix)
Department of Health
Vital Statistics
Charles Harwood Memorial
Complex
Christiansted, St. Croix, VI 00820

Virgin Islands (St. Thomas, St. John)
Department of Health
Vital Statistics
Old Municipal Hospital
St. Thomas, VI 00802

Hague Convention Nations

The nations listed on the following pages are parties to a treaty called the *Hague Convention Abolishing the Requirement of Legalization* (Authentication) *for Foreign Public Documents.*

Treaty Simplifies Authentication. A Notary's signature on documents that are sent to these nations may be authenticated by the Washington Department of Licensing through attachment of a single certificate of capacity called an *apostille.* The *apostille* (French for "notation") is the only authentication certificate necessary. Nations not subscribing to the Hague Convention may require as many as five or six separate authenticating certificates from different governmental agencies, domestic and foreign.

How to Request an *Apostille.* To obtain an *apostille,* mail or present in person a written request, the original notarized document, the Notary's name, the Notary's commission expiration date and a $15 fee per document in a check payable to the "Washington State Treasurer" to:

Department of Licensing
Notary Public Licensing Department
P.O. Box 9048 (405 Black Lake Blvd. S.W.)
Olympia, WA 98507-9048
(360) 664-1550

An *apostille* must be specifically requested, indicating the nation to which the document will be sent.

It is not the Notary's responsibility to obtain an *apostille.* It is the responsibility of the party sending the document.

Hague Convention Nations. The following nations participate in the Hague Convention:

Albania	Fiji[10]
Andorra[10]	Finland
Antigua and Barbuda[10]	France[3]
Argentina[1]	Georgia
Armenia[10]	Germany
Australia	Greece
Austria	Grenada[10]
Azerbajian	Honduras[10]
Bahamas[10]	Hong Kong[4]
Barbados[10]	Hungary
Belarus	Iceland
Belgium	India
Belize[10]	Ireland
Bosnia-Herzegovina[2]	Israel
Botswana[10]	Italy
Brunei Darussalam[10]	Japan
Bulgaria	Kazakhstan[10]
Colombia[10]	Latvia
Cook Islands	Lesotho[10]
Croatia[2]	Liberia[5, 10]
Cyprus	Liechtenstein[10]
Czech Republic	Lithuania
Denmark	Luxembourg
Dominica[10]	Macao[4]
Ecuador	Macedonia[2]
El Salvador[10]	Malawi[10]
Estonia	Malta

1. Excludes recognition of extension of the Convention by the United Kingdom to the Malvinas (Falkland Islands), South Georgia, South Sandwich Islands and the Argentine Antarctic Sector.

2. The former Yugoslavia was a party to the Convention. Only the breakaway nations of Bosnia-Herzegovina, Croatia, Macedonia, Serbia and Montenegro and Slovenia have confirmed that the Convention still applies.

3. Including *Comoros Islands, Djibouti*, French Guyana, French Polynesia, Guadeloupe, Martinique, New Caledonia, Reunion, St. Pierre and Miquelon, and Wallis and Futuna. (Names appearing in regular type denote territories; *italic type denotes now-independent nations that have not affirmed participation in the Convention.*)

4. Retained status as Hague nation after control was returned to China on July 1, 1997 (Hong Kong) and December 20, 1999 (Macao).

5. Convention does not apply between Liberia and the U.S. Liberia is a nonmember of the Convention which is a contracting state or has signed to the Convention.

Marshall Islands[10]
Mauritius[10]
Mexico
Moldova
Monaco
Namibia[10]
Netherlands[6]
New Zealand
Niue[10]
North Korea
Norway
Panama
Poland
Portugal[7]
Romania
Russian Federation
Saint Kitts and Nevis[10]
Saint Lucia[10]
Saint Vincent and
the Grenadines[10]

Samoa[10]
San Marino[10]
Serbia and Montenegro[2]
Seychelles
Slovakia
Slovenia[2]
South Africa
Spain
Suriname
Swaziland[10]
Sweden
Switzerland
Tonga[10]
Trinidad and Tobago[10]
Turkey
Ukraine
United Kingdom[8]
United States[9]
Venezuela

Inquiries. Persons having questions about the *Hague Convention Abolishing the Requirement of Legalization for Foreign Public Documents* may address their inquiries to:

Authentication Office
518 23rd Street, N.W.
State Annex 1
Washington, DC 20037
(202) 647-5002

6. Extended to all Aruba, Curacao and Netherlands Antilles.

7. Extended to Angola, Mozambique and all overseas territories.

8. United Kingdom of Great Britain and Northern Ireland is extended to Anguilla, Bermuda, British Antarctica Territory, British Virgin Islands, Cayman Islands, Falkland Islands, Gibraltar, Guyana, Guernsey, Isle of Man Jersey, *Kiribati,* Montserrat, St. Helena, Solomon Islands, Turks and Caicos Islands, *Tuvalu, Vanuatu* and *Zimbabwe.* (Names appearing in regular type denote territories; *italic type denotes now-independent nations that have not affirmed participation in the Convention.*)

9. Includes American Samoa, District of Columbia, Guam, Northern Mariana Islands, Puerto Rico and U.S. Virgin Islands.

10. Nonmember of the Convention which is a contracting state or has signed to the Convention. ∎

About the NNA

Since 1957, the nonprofit National Notary Association has served the nation's Notaries Public — today numbering over four and a half million — with a wide variety of instructional programs and services.

As the country's clearinghouse for information on notarial laws, customs and practices, the NNA educates Notaries through publications, seminars, annual conferences and a Notary Information Service Hotline that offers immediate answers to specific questions about notarization.

The Association is perhaps most widely known as the preeminent publisher of information for and about Notaries. NNA works include:

- *The National Notary*, a magazine for National Notary Association members featuring how-to articles and practical tips on notarizing.

- *Notary Bulletin* newspaper, keeping NNA members up to date on developments affecting Notaries, especially new state laws and regulations.

- *Notary Basics Made Easy*, a first-of-its-kind video instruction program that simplifies Notary practices and procedures.

- *Notary Home Study Course*, a work-at-your-own-speed course covering every facet of notarization.

- *Sorry, No Can Do!* series, four volumes that help Notaries explain to customers and bosses why some requests for notarizations are improper and cannot be accommodated.

- *U.S. Notary Reference Manual*, invaluable for any person relying upon the authenticity and correctness of legal documents.

- *Notary Public Practices & Glossary*, widely hailed as the Notary's bible, a definitive reference book on notarial procedures.

- *State Notary Law Primers*, explaining a state's notarial statutes in easy-to-understand language.

- *NSA Q&A*, providing real-world answers to the Notary Signing Agent's most-asked questions.

- *The Complete Handbook of Loan Documents and Transactions*, the Notary Signing Agent's illustrated guide to common and uncommon forms and how to notarize them.

- *Model Notary Act*, prototype legislation conceived in 1973 and updated in 1984 and 2002 by an NNA-recruited panel of secretaries of state, legislators, and attorneys, and regularly used by state legislatures in revising their notarial laws.

- *Notary Law & Practice: Cases & Materials*, the definitive and one-of-a-kind text for teaching Notary law to law students in schools and to attorneys in Minimum Continuing Education Seminars (MCLE), discussing every major judicial decision affecting the Notary's duties.

- *Notary Signing Agent Certification Course*, invaluable for candidates preparing to complete the Notary Signing Agent Certification Examination developed by the National Notary Association.

- Public-service pamphlets informing the general public about the function of a Notary — including *What Is A Notary Public?* — printed in English and Spanish.

In addition, the National Notary Association offers the highest quality professional supplies, including official seals and stamps, embossers, recordkeeping journals, affidavit stamps, thumbprinting devices and notarial certificates.

Though dedicated primarily to educating and assisting Notaries, the National Notary Association devotes part of its resources to helping lawmakers draft effective notarial statutes and to informing the public about the Notary's vital role in modern society. ■

Index

A

Acknowledgment. . 22, **23-28**, *80, 100*
  Acknowledge signature. 24
  Capacity of signer 24-25
  Certificates for **25-27**, 47, *81-82*
  Common act. 23
  Defined *78*
  Disabled signer, taking for *100*
  Fee **52**
  Identifying signer 24, 25, 27
  Personal appearance. 24
  Purpose 24
  Requirements 24
  Terminology. 27
  Who may take **27-28**, *83-84*
               97-98, 99-100
  Witnessing signature 11-12, **27**
Act, certifying 23, **35-36**, *80*
  Certificate for **36**, 48, *83*
  Document required 36
  Fee *104*
  Procedures. 36
  Purpose. 35-36
Address, change of. 21, *105*
Affirmations 22, **30-32**, *87-88*
  Ceremony and gestures 32
  Corporate oaths 31
  Credible identifying witness, for . 41
  Defined 30
  Equivalent to oath *88*
  Fee. 52, *104*

Jurat, for 32-33
Power to administer . **31**, *87-88, 100*
Purpose. 30-31
Response required 31-32
Subscribing witness, for 35
Verification, for 32-33
Wording. *88*
Apostille **59**, *84-85, 113*
Application. 3-4, **18-19**, *104*
  Completing 4
  Endorsements 4, **19**, *78-79*
  Fee **19**, *79, 104*
  Obtaining. 3
  Personal declaration 20, *79*
  Reappointment 4, **22**, *80, 104*
  Rejection of 19
  Submitting 4
Authentication. **58**, *84-85, 105*
                113-114
  Apostille. 59, *84, 85*
  Certificates of authority. 58, *85*
  Certificates of capacity 58
  Certificates of official character . . 58
  Fee 58
  Flags 58
  Hague Convention Abolishing
    the Requirement of
    Legalization for Foreign
    Public Documents 59, *85*
                113-115

Page numbers listed in **bold** indicate where the most complete information on a subject can be found. *Italics* indicate the pages where the statutes pertaining to a subject are located.

Military personnel, of 62
Out of country. 58-59
Out of state 58

B

Beneficial interest. 12, **53**
Birth certificates, certifying
  copies of **11**, 29, 109
Blank spaces in documents . 14-15, **54**
Bond, Notary. 4, **19-20**, *79*
  Liability 20
  Purpose 20
Bureaus of Vital Statistics 109-112

C

Capacity of signer . . . 15, 24-25, 25-26
  39, 43
Certificates, notarial 7, 16, 25-27
  32-33, 33-34, 35, 37-38, **44-49**
  62-63, 81-83, 88, 105
  Acknowledgment, for . . . **25-27**, 47
  81-82, 97-98, 99
  Attorney in fact, for 26, *82*
  Certified copy, for . . . **29**, 48, *82-83*
  Certifying act or event. . . 36, 48, *83*
  Choosing/Selecting 16, 17, **46**
  105
  Contents 44-45
  Correcting 10
  Deposition, for. 30
  Disabled signer, for 56-57
  False **49**, 65, *84*, 88-89, *91*
  Format requirements **44-45**, *81*
  Illegible 49
  Jurat, for **32-33**, 48, *82*
  Loose 16-17, **45**
  Military personnel, and 61-62
  Pre-sign or pre-seal 46-47
  Proof of acknowledgment by
    subscribing witness 35
  Protest, for. 37-38
  Requirement. **44**, *81*
  Seal/stamp of Notary 45
  Short-form certificates 26-27
  47-48, *81-83*
  Signature of Notary. 44
  Size requirements . . **45-46**, *102-103*
  Statement of particulars 44
  Telegraphic copies 49, *88*
  Testimonium clause 44

Venue 44
Verification upon oath or
  affirmation **32-33**, 48, *82*
Wills, for 62-63
Witnessing signatures,
  for **33-34**, 48, *82*
Certified copies 11, 22, **28-29**, *80*
  Birth certificate, of 11, **29**
  Certificate for. 29, 48, *82-83*
  Death certificate, of 11, **29**
  Fee 52
  Precautions 29
  Procedure 28-29, *80*
  Purpose 28
  Recordable documents 28
  Vital records, of 11, **29**
Commission, Notary . . **18-22**, *104-105*
  Address, change of. 21, *105*
  Application, rejection of 19
  Bond. 4, **19-20**, *79*
  Certificate of appointment 79
  Denial of 19, *79*
  Endorsements 19, *78-79*
  Fee 19
  Jurisdiction. 20, *80*
  Name, change of 21-22, *105*
  Oath for. 4, **20**, *79*
  Personal declaration 20, *79*
  Qualifications 3, **18**, *78-79*
  Rejection of application 19
  Renewal. 4, *80*
  Resignation **21**, *85, 106*
  Revocation 64, *84-85*
  Term of office 20, *80*
Conformed copies 10
Credible identifying
  witness. 9, 31, **40-41**, *81*
  Affirmation for 31, **41**
  Identification of 40-41
  Journal entry 41
  Oath for. 31, **41**
  Purpose 40
  Qualifications . . . 9, **40-41**, *81, 106*
  Subscribing witness, confusion
    with. 41
Customers, limiting
  services to. 10-11

D

Date of document 15

Department of Licensing. . . 3, 58, *103*
                                    108
Deposition. 22, **30**
  Affirmation for **30**, 31
  Definition. 30
  Oath for. **30**, 31
  Purpose 30
Digital signatures. 69-70
  Electronic notarization 69
  Electronic transactions 69
  Uniform Real Property Electronic
     Recording Act 70, *100-102*
Disabled signer, signing
  for **56-57**, *80, 100*
  Certificate. **56**, *80, 100*
  Journal entry 57
  Notarization 56
Disqualifying interest . 9, 34, 41, **53-54**
  Financial interest 53
  Impartiality. 53
  Relatives. 12, **54**
Documents
  Blank spaces **14-15**, 54
  Date, checking 15
  False 65
  Foreign language 11, **60**
  Immigration. 60-61
  Incomplete **14-15**, 54
  Notarial wording, checking for . . 16
  Preparation of 17, **55**
  Scan for information 15
  Signed in Notary's presence . . 11-12
Duties **22-23**, *78, 80-81*

E

Electronic notarization 69
Electronic transactions 69
Embosser 6, **49-50**
Employer/Notary relationship 55
Equipment. 6
Errors and omissions insurance 7
Event, certifying. . . . 23, **35-36**, *80, 83*
  Certificate for **36**, 48, *83*
  Document required 36
  Fee *104*
  Procedures. 36

Purpose. 35-36
Exam, trial. 71-76

F

Family members, notarizing
  for. 12, **54**
Fees. **52**, *83, 104*
  Ackowledgments, for 52
  Affirmation, for. 52, *104*
  Authentication, for 58
  Certified copy, for 52
  Certifying event or act, for *104*
  Failure to post 66
  Journal entry 43
  Jurat, for 52
  Maximum. 52, *104*
  Oath, for 52, *104*
  Option not to charge . . 53, *81, 104*
  Overcharging 53, 66
  Posting. 53, *104*
  Proof of acknowledgment, for . . 52
  Protest, for 52, *104*
  Travel 52-53, *104*
  Verification, for. 52
  Witnessing signature, for. 52
Financial interest 12, **53**
Foreign languages 11, **59-60**
  Advertising 59-60
  Documents. 11, **60**
  Signers. 60
  Translate "Notary Public" 60

H

Hague Convention Abolishing
  the Requirement of
  Legalization for Foreign
  Public Documents. 59, **113-115**

I

Identification 9, 13, **38-41**, *106*
  Acknowledgments, for 38, *106*
  Checking signatures 14
  Credible identifying
    witness 9, 38, **40-41**, *106*
  ID cards 38, **39-40**, *106*
  Journal entry 42-43

Page numbers listed in **bold** indicate where the most complete information on a subject can be found. *Italics* indicate the pages where the statutes pertaining to a subject are located.

Jurats, for 38
Minors, of 57-58
Other notarial acts, for 38-39
Personal knowledge 38, **39**
Proof of representative capacity . 39
Verification, for 38
Witnessing signatures, for 38
Identification documents . . 39-40, *106*
Acceptable 39, *106*
Fraudulent 40
Multiple 39-40
Immigration 60-61
Advice 60
Documents 60-61
Naturalization certificates 61, 66
Impartiality 9, 12, 36, 41, **53-54**
Incomplete documents 14-15, **54**
Insurance, errors and omissions 7
Investigation and appeal . . 67-68, *105*

J

Journal of notarial acts . 6-7, 15, **41-44**
Complete before certificate 15
Copies of entries 43
Credible identifying witness,
and 41
Death of Notary, and 67
Disabled signer, with 57
Entries 42-43
Never surrender 44
Recommendation 41-42
Signature by mark, entry for 57
Subscribing witness, and 35
Thumbprint 7
Jurat 7, 22, **32-33**, *80*
Affirmation 32, **33**
Certificate **32-33**, 48, *82*
Defined *78*
Fee **52**
Identification 32
Oath 32, **33**
Part of verification 32
Purpose 32
Sign in Notary's presence 32
Stamp 7
Jurisdiction 20, *80*

L

Law, unauthorized
practice of 17, **55**, 62, 65
86-87, *105*

Advice and assistance 17, **55**
60, 62, *105*
Blanks in document 14-15, **55**
Exceptions 55, *105*
Preparing document . . . 17, **55**, *105*
Selecting notarization 17, *105*
Wills, and 62
Laws pertaining to notarization . *77-107*
Liability of Notary 20, 67
Living wills 63
Locus sigilli (L.S.) **45**, 50
Loose certificates 16-17, **45**

M

Marriages 23, **57**, *90*
Military-personnel notarizations . 61-62
Authentication 62
Certificate 61-62
Jurisdiction 61
Who are authorized 61
Minors, notarizing for 57-58
Identification 57-58
Signature 57
Misconduct **63-68**, *84, 90-92*
Action on other professional
license 64
Defined 63, *90*
Denial of appointment 63, 79
Duty performed by another 66
Endorsement 66, *106*
Endorsements and
testimonials 66, *106*
Failure to perform duty . . 66, *91-92*
False certificate 65, *84*
False document, completing 65
Fees, failure to post 66
Felony conviction 64-65, *106*
Forgery *89*
Impersonating a Notary . . 65, *84, 89*
Judged incompetent 64
Law, unauthorized practice
of 17, **55**, 62, 65
86-87
Liability for damages **20**, 67
Naturalization certificate,
copying or notarizing 66
Overcharging 66, *89-90*
Personal Appearance,
failure to require 65
Qualification, failure to
maintain 63-65, *106*

Revocation of appointment . . 64, *83*
Seal/Stamp,
  disposition of 66-67, *105*
Seal/Stamp, manufacturing of . . . 67
Serious crime 63, *78*
Signature under
  duress 66, *89*
Unlawful compensation,
  requesting *89-90*

N

Name, change of 21-22
                                      103-105
National Notary Association . . 116-117
Naturalization certificates **61**, 66
Notarial acts **22-38**, *78, 80-81*
  Acknowledgment . . . 22 , **23-28**, *80*
  Act, certifying 23, **35-36**, *80*
  Affirmations 22, **30-32**, *78*
  Certified copies 11, 22, **28-29**
                                   80, 82-83
  Defined *78*
  Deposition 22, **30**
  Event, certifying 23, **35-36**, *80*
  Jurat 22, **32-33**, *80*
  Oaths 22, **30-32**, *78, 87-88*
  Proof of acknowledgment
    by subscribing witness . 23, **34-35**
  Unauthorized acts 23
  Verification upon oath or
    affirmation 22, **32-33**, *80*
  Witnessing signatures . 23, 33-34, *80*
Notarial certifcates (see
  Certificates, notarial)
Notarial records (see
  Journal of notarial acts)
Notario Publico/Notaria Publica . . . 60
Notary seal (See Seal/Stamp, Notary)

O

Oath of office, Notary's 4
Oaths 22, **30-32**, *78, 87-88*
  Ceremony and gestures 32
  Corporate oaths 31
  Credible identifying witness, for . 41
  Defined 30

Fee 52, *104*
Power to administer . **31**, *87-88*, *100*
Purpose 30-31
Response required 31-32
Subscribing witness, for 35
Wordings 31, *87*

P

Penalties 63-68, *84, 89-92*
Personal appearance . . . **13**, 32, 33, 65
Personal declaration 20, *79*
Personal knowledge
  of identity 39, *80-81*
  Defined 39
Photocopies, notarizing 10
Photographs, notarizing 9
Proof of acknowledgment by
  subscribing witness 23, **34-35**
  Affirmation for 35
  Certificate for 35
  Fee 52
  Identification 35
  In lieu of acknowledgment 34
  Oath for 35
  Purpose 34
  Signing journal 35
  Subscribing witness 34
Protest 23, **36-38**, *80, 92-97*
  Affidavit of service by mail . . 38, *97*
  Antiquated act 37
  Certificate for 37-38, *96*
  Fees 52, *104*
  Purpose 36-37
  Special knowledge required 37

Q

Qualifications 3, **18**, *78-79, 106*

R

Reasonable care 13-17, **54**
Refusal of services 54
Representative capacity, defined . . . *78*
Resignation **21**, *84-85, 104*
  Disposition of seal 51, *104*
  Procedure 21
  Purpose 21

Page numbers listed in **bold** indicate where the most complete information on a subject can be found. *Italics* indicate the pages where the statutes pertaining to a subject are located.

Restricting services. 10-11
Revised Code of Washington
(RCW) (See Washington,
Revised Code of) *77-107*

S

Satisfactory evidence. 24, *81, 106*
Scilicet (SS., SCT.). 44
Seal/Stamp, Notary 5, 6, 16, 45
49-51, *66-67, 80-81, 103-105*
Affixing 16
Authorization to
purchase 50
Death of Notary, and 67
Disposition of **51**, 66-67
Embosser **6**, 49, 50
Exclusive property
of Notary 51, **67**, *81*
Expired seal 50, *106*
Format 49, *103*
Lost or stolen 51, *105*
Manufacturing of. **50**, 67, *103*
Name change, with . . . 22, *103-104*
No room for 9-10
Placement of 50
Preprinted 51
Property of Notary 51
Required information 49-50
Requirement. 49, *80*
Resignation, and. 67
Smearing. 9-10
State seal 50
Using to endorse 23
Secretary of State's office. . . 3, 58, 108
Self-notarization 23, **65**, *81*
Serious crime defined. 63, *78*
Signature by Mark 55-56
Procedures. 56
Witnesses. 56
Signature, Notary's 16, **44,** *106*
Notarizing one's own 23, *81*
Under duress 66, *89*
Statement of particulars 44
Statutes pertaining to
notarization *77-107*
Subscribing witness 23, **34-35**
Supplies 6-7
Surety 20, *79*

T

Telephone notarizations . . . 13, **23**, 24
Term of office, Notary's 20, *78*
Testimonium clause 44
Thumbprint 7
Tools, Notary 6-7

U

U.S. Code:
Title 10, Section 936 62
Title 10, Section 1044a 62
Unauthorized acts 23
Uniform Real Property Electronic
Recording Act 70, *100-102*

V

Venue 7, **44**
Stamp 7
Verification upon oath
or affirmation 22, **32-33**, *80*
Affirmation. 32, **33**
Certificate 32-33, *82*
Defined *78*
Fee 52
Identification **32**, 48, *80*
Oath 32, **33**
Purpose 32
Sign in Notary's presence 32
Vital records, notarizing 11, **29**
Vital Statistics, Bureaus of. . . . 109-112

W

Washington Administrative Code (WAC)
308-30-005 . . . . *103*
308-30-010 . . . . 22, 49, 50
51, 67, *103-104*
308-30-020. . . . . 52, 53, 66, *104*
308-30-030 . . . . *104*
308-30-040. . . . . 21, 51, 67, *104*
308-30-050 . . . . 51, *105*
308-30-060 . . . . . . ·. . . . 21, 22, *105*
308-30-070 . . . . 58, 59, *105*
308-30-080 . . . . 68, *105*
308-30-090. . . . . 46, 55, 60, 65, *105*
308-30-100. . . . . . . 19, 22, 50, *105*
308-30-120 . . . . 44, *106*
308-30-130 . . . . 50, *106*
308-30-140 . . . . 65, *106*
308-30-150 . . . . 21, 64, *106*
308-30-155. . . . . . . 38, 39, 40, *106*

308-30-160. . . . . . . 23, 36, 66, *106*
308-30-170 . . . . *106*
308-30-180 . . . . *107*
308-30-190 . . . . *107*
Washington, Revised Code of (RCW):
2.48.170 . . . . 55, 65, *86*
2.48.180 . . . . 55, 65, *86*
5.28.010 . . . . 30, *87*
5.28.020 . . . . 30, *87*
5.28.030 . . . . *87*
5.28.040 . . . . 30, *88*
5.28.050 . . . . *86, 88*
5.28.060 . . . . *88*
5.52.050 . . . . 49, *88*
9A.60.010 . . . . *88*
9A.60.020 . . . . 49, 65, *89*
9A.60.030 . . . . 66, *89*
9A.60.040 . . . . *89*
9A.60.050 . . . . *89*
9A.68.020 . . . . 53, 66, *89-90*
9A.80.010 . . . . 66, *90*
26.04.150 . . . . 57, *90*
36.18.010 . . . . *90*
42.20.020 . . . . 66, *91*
42.20.030 . . . . *91*
42.20.040 . . . . *91*
42.20.050 . . . . 49, 65, *91*
42.20.100 . . . . 54, *91-92*
42.44.010 . . . . 22, 24, 25, 28, 31
     32, 39, 63, *78*
42.44.020 . . . . 18, 19, 20, 21, *78-79*
42.44.030 . . . . . . 18-19, 63, 64, *79*
42.44.040 . . . . *79*
42.44.050 . . . . 49, 67, *80*
42.44.060 . . . . 20, *80*
42.44.070 . . . . 19, *80*
42.44.080 . . . . 22-24, 27, 29
     32-33, 36, 38-40, 53, 56, *80-81*
42.44.090 . . . . 44, 49, 51, 55, 67, *81*
42.44.100 . . . . 25, 26, 29, 32-33
     36, 47, 75, *81-83*
42.44.110 . . . . 49, 75, *83*
42.44.120 . . . . 53, 75, *83*
42.44.130 . . . . 28, 75, 78, *83*

42.44.140 . . . . 75, 78, *83-84*
42.44.150 . . . . 75, *84*
42.44.160 . . . . . . 49, 63, 65, 75, *84*
42.44.170 . . . . . . 21, 64, 75, *84-85*
42.44.180 . . . . 58, 59, 75, *85*
42.44.190 . . . . *76, 85*
42.44.200 . . . . *85*
42.44.900 . . . . *76, 85*
42.44.901 . . . . *76, 85*
42.44.902 . . . . *76, 85*
42.44.903 . . . . *76, 86*
62A.3-501 . . . . 37, *92*
62A.3-502 . . . . *92-94*
62A.3-503 . . . . 37, *94*
62A.3-504 . . . . *94-95*
62A.3-505 . . . . 37, *95*
62A.3-512 . . . . *95*
62A.3-515 . . . . *95-96*
62A.3-520 . . . . 37, 38, *96-97*
62A.3-522 . . . . 37, 38, *97*
62A.3-525 . . . . *97*
64.08.010 . . . . 27, *97*
64.08.020 . . . . 28, *97-98*
64.08.040 . . . . 28, *98*
64.08.050 . . . . *98*
64.08.060 . . . . 25, *98-99*
64.08.070 . . . . 25, *99*
64.08.090 . . . . 27, *99-100*
64.08.100 . . . . 56, 57, 78, *100*
65.04.045 . . . . 46, *102-103*
Weddings 23, **57**, *90*
Willingness, determining 13-14
Wills 8, **62-63**
  Advice and assistance 62
  Certificate 62-63
  Law, unauthorized practice of . . . 62
  Living Wills 63
Witnessing signatures . . 23, **33-34**, *80*
  Certificate **33-34**, 48, *82*
  Fee **52**
  Identification 33
  Purpose **33**, *80*
  Signed in Notary's presence 33

Page numbers listed in **bold** indicate where the most complete information on a subject can be found. *Italics* indicate the pages where the statutes pertaining to a subject are located.